LEADING WOMEN

Democratic
Campaigner
and Advocate

Chelsea Clinton

CATHLEEN SMALL

Cavendish
Square

New York

Published in 2018 by Cavendish Square Publishing, LLC
243 5th Avenue, Suite 136, New York, NY 10016

Copyright © 2018 by Cavendish Square Publishing, LLC

First Edition

Library of Congress Cataloging-in-Publication Data

Names: Small, Cathleen, author.
Title: Chelsea Clinton : democratic campaigner and advocate / Cathleen Small.
Description: New York : Cavendish Square Publishing, 2018. | Series: Leading
women | Includes bibliographical references and index.
Identifiers: LCCN 2017015902 (print) | LCCN 2017020458 (ebook) | ISBN
9781502631732 (E-book) | ISBN 9781502631725 (library bound) | ISBN 9781502634115 (pbk.)
Subjects: LCSH: Clinton, Chelsea--Juvenile literature. | Children of
presidents--United States--Juvenile literature.
Classification: LCC E887.C5 (ebook) | LCC E887.C5 S63 2018 (print) | DDC
973.929092 [B] --dc23
LC record available at https://lccn.loc.gov/2017015902

Editorial Director: David McNamara
Editor: Jodyanne Benson
Copy Editor: Nathan Heidelberger
Associate Art Director: Amy Greenan
Designer: Renni Johnson
Production Coordinator: Karol Szymczuk
Photo Research: J8 Media

The photographs in this book are used by permission and through the courtesy of: LW-Chelsea
Clinton credits. Photo credits: Cover J. Countess/Getty Images; p. 1, 54 Sonia Recchia/WireImage/
Getty Images; p. 4 Cynthia Johnson/The LIFE Images Collection/Getty Images; p. 7 Wellesley
College/Sygma/Getty Images; p. 11 Danny Johnston/Getty Images; p. 12 Smith Collection/Gado/
Getty Images; p. 18 Lou DeMatteis/Reuters/Alamy Stock Photo; p. 21 Cynthia Johnson/Getty
Images; p. 27 Roberto Borea/AP Images; p. 30 Dave Benett/Getty Images; p. 32 Mike Coppola/
Getty Images; p. 34 Alex Wong/Getty Images; p. 37, 44 Zuma Press/Alamy Stock Photo; p. 40
Michael Loccisano/Getty Images; p. 48 Johnny Louis/FilmMagic/Getty Images; p. 50 Paul Morigi/
WireImage/Getty Images; p. 57 FilmMagic/Getty Images; p. 64 Kevin Winter/Getty Images; p. 68
Polaris Images/Newscom; p. 73 Silvia Izquierdo/AP Images; p. 79 Doug Mills/AP Images; p. 80 Star
Max/IPx/AP Images; p. 87 Brooks Kraft/Getty Images.

Printed in the United States of America

CONTENTS

CHAPTER ONE

From Little Rock to the White House

C helsea Clinton entered the public eye at the age of twelve, when her father, Bill, took office as the forty-second president of the United States. Previously, Bill Clinton had been governor of Arkansas, so Chelsea was in the public eye to some extent pretty much since birth—in fact, she appeared on the front page of an Arkansas newspaper shortly after she was born. But it was at age twelve, on the cusp of entering her teen years, that Chelsea became a household name.

Chelsea Clinton at 12 years old

Growing Up Clinton

Chelsea might never have been known as anything other than a bright, inquisitive child of the 1980s if it weren't for her **pedigree**. Before he became president of the United States, Bill Clinton was the governor of Arkansas from 1979 to 1981, and then again from 1983 to 1992.

Before becoming governor, Bill Clinton earned a law degree from Yale Law School. After graduating, he taught law at the University of Arkansas. He became active in politics not long after graduating from Yale, leading George McGovern's presidential campaign in Texas in 1972 and working with Texas politicians Ron Kirk (later mayor of Dallas) and Ann Richards (later governor of Texas). After returning to Arkansas, Clinton ran for the House of Representatives as a Democrat, but he lost to Republican John Paul Hammerschmidt. Not letting the defeat dissuade him, he ran for Arkansas attorney general in 1976 and won the election. When he was elected governor in 1978, he became the United States' youngest governor.

In 1975, Bill Clinton married Hillary Rodham, whom he had met while a student at Yale Law School, where she was also studying law. The two were a power couple from the start. Hillary was actually a year ahead of Bill at Yale. She graduated in 1973 and went on to serve as a congressional legal counsel.

Bill Clinton and Hillary Rodham in 1979

A Chicago native, Hillary moved with Bill to Arkansas not long before their marriage. There, like Bill, she taught law at the University of Arkansas. In 1977, she cofounded Arkansas Advocates for Children and Families, a nonprofit organization that advocates for policies to benefit children and families. The next year, she became the first female chair of the Legal Services Corporation. In 1979, she became the first female partner at Rose Law Firm.

The vast majority of Hillary's legal work during those early years in Arkansas focused on children's law and family policy. She authored numerous scholarly articles about topics surrounding children's legal rights, which earned her a reputation as an important scholar and activist.

Needless to say, when Chelsea Victoria Clinton entered the world on February 27, 1980, she was born to two very busy, very successful, but also very doting parents.

An Arkansas Childhood

Chelsea was born during her father's first term as governor of Arkansas. She was an only child, and her parents were strict but also loving. Chelsea was not allowed to eat sugary cereals for breakfast, and pizza was a treat saved for weekends. She was allowed only thirty minutes of television per day.

Although both of her parents worked in high-powered jobs, family mealtime was a priority. Bill Clinton ate breakfast with Chelsea every morning, and over dinner the family of three would come together to discuss everything from news and the media to movies, television shows, and computer games. In 2012, reflecting on her childhood, Chelsea said, "Those conversations helped me develop a broad and healthy skepticism about the media as well as a respect for its ability … to empower or disempower people."[1]

The conversations also helped Chelsea develop the thick skin needed to survive in the public eye. She remembers, at age six, her family having mock debates at the dinner table, as preparation for Bill's 1986 **gubernatorial** race. Bill and Hillary knew that Chelsea would undoubtedly hear negative things about her father during the race, and they wanted to prepare her for that.

In her book *It Takes a Village*, Hillary describes how Chelsea "gradually gained mastery over her emotions" thanks in part to these mock debates.[2] That composure, learned early on over dinner-table debates, would serve Chelsea well twelve years later, when her father faced harsh criticism and possible impeachment as president of the United States, and the nation looked to Chelsea's response to guide their own reactions toward the scandal. As Chelsea told *Vogue* in 2012, "Having thick skin is an important quality for anyone who wants to do something in the world, and thankfully that's something I had to develop early on."[3]

Video games were allowed in the Clinton home, but only as a family activity. Chelsea remembers playing computer games *Oregon Trail* and *Carmen San Diego* with her father. But video games were just one family activity. Chelsea and her father also enjoyed cowriting stories. Chelsea would write the first paragraph of a story, and then Bill would write the second. Chelsea would take the third, Bill the fourth, and so on until the story was complete.

Ritual was a big part of the Clinton family. Chelsea told *Vogue* in 2012 about some of her memories of growing up in Arkansas:

Sundays were really sacred times. We would go to church, have lunch, and we always did something new, whether it was crack open coconuts or go on a new hike. We had these rituals that rooted us very much together ... There was a real effort from [my parents]. They organized their lives so that we could have that time. Even during my father's first campaign for president, there were only three nights when I wasn't with one or both of them.[4]

Chelsea also enjoyed ballet dancing. Because of her parents' busy work schedules, her grandparents or babysitters often had to take her to lessons, which she began at the age of four. Her mother, though, was very open about her belief that it takes a village to raise a child—the sentiment even inspired the title of Hillary's 1996 book. But the village who helped raise Chelsea never took the place of Chelsea's parents. Bill set up a desk for Chelsea in his office so they could spend time together, and Hillary would help out on class field trips and would interrupt her daily schedule to talk to her daughter when Chelsea arrived home from school.

Though she grew up in the luxurious Governor's Mansion in Little Rock, Arkansas, Chelsea attended public schools, including Forest Park Elementary. She was a bright student who earned high marks and skipped third grade. By the time she was eleven, Chelsea had learned how to invest in the stock market. She had also learned that she no longer wanted to eat meat, having read about the negative effects red meat can have on the body, so she became a vegetarian. Chelsea learned determination from both of her parents, but especially from her mother, whom she credits as an inspiration. In

Eleven-year-old Chelsea with her parents in Little Rock, Arkansas

a post for PopSugar, Chelsea wrote, "My mom has been my hero for my whole life. I remember watching how hard she worked when I was growing up and thinking she could do anything."[5]

Moving to the White House

Having grown up in the spotlight, Chelsea knew having a thick skin was essential to survival. When her father assumed the presidency in early 1993, Chelsea was just about to turn thirteen. It's an awkward age for many people, and Chelsea was no exception. She had a mop of unruly strawberry hair and a mouth full of braces.

The standard preteen awkwardness became all the more cutting when Chelsea was publicly mocked by

Chelsea plays with Socks the cat in the Oval Office on Christmas Eve 1994.

Rush Limbaugh, a conservative radio host, as well as on *Saturday Night Live*. Limbaugh publicly referred to Chelsea as "the White House dog" just days after her father's election. Shortly thereafter, *Saturday Night Live* did a "Wayne's World" sketch in which comedian Mike Myers asserted that "adolescence has been thus far unkind" to Chelsea. When Chelsea was eighteen, Senator John McCain reportedly mocked her appearance at a fundraising dinner in Arizona by telling the joke: "Do you know why Chelsea Clinton is so ugly? Because [Attorney General] Janet Reno is her father."[6]

Her parents had her back, though. First Lady Hillary Clinton publicly criticized *Saturday Night Live* for the jokes, which prompted a public apology from the show's executive producer, Lorne Michaels, who said, "We felt, upon reflection, that if it was in any way hurtful, it wasn't worth it. She's a kid, a kid who didn't choose to be in public life."[7] And Mike Myers wrote a letter of apology to the White House.

It wasn't just Hillary who had her daughter's back, though. Bill did as well. In an interview shortly after the Limbaugh and *Saturday Night Live* jabs, the president said of the attacks on his daughter's appearance:

I think there is something pretty off-center with people who do that. But I've determined that I can't control their behavior, so I'll just have to control our response to it. We really work hard on making sure that Chelsea doesn't let other people define her sense of her own self-worth. I think the world would be a lot better off if more people were to define themselves in terms of their own standards and values and not what other people said or thought about them. It's tough when you are an adolescent because peer opinion and other people's opinion become more important. But I think she'll be okay.[8]

After the initial comments about Chelsea, media commentary about her tapered off, mostly because her parents established an informal agreement with the press that Chelsea was off limits. The two of them had signed up for life in the public eye, but Chelsea had

Standing Up for White House Kids

Chelsea grew into a confident, accomplished young woman, despite the challenges she faced as an adolescent. In 2017, when she saw President Trump's son Barron receive the same type of mocking she had received twenty-five years earlier, Chelsea stepped up and reprimanded people in a tweet: "Barron Trump deserves the chance every child does—to be a kid."[9]

Chelsea may have been a surprising defender of young Barron, given that his father had just defeated her mother, Hillary Rodham Clinton, in an incredibly bitter battle for the presidency. Indeed, Chelsea's tweet also included a thinly veiled commentary on President Trump's policies, saying, "Standing up for every kid also means opposing @POTUS policies that hurt kids."[10]

Political differences aside, Chelsea is, at heart, a compassionate human being and friend. She and First Daughter Ivanka Trump have long been friends, and Chelsea said in a 2015 interview, "Friendship is always more important than politics. I learned that growing up, watching my parents be friends with people across the political spectrum in Arkansas."[11]

not—and the Clintons wanted the media to respect that. Hillary Clinton's deputy press secretary at the time, Neel Lattimore, stated in summer 1993, "The president and First Lady have made it very clear they want Chelsea to have as normal a life as possible."[12]

After President Clinton's first month in the White House, when more than 1,200 newspaper and magazine articles mentioned Chelsea, the mentions slowed to 400 articles in February 1993, fewer than 300 in April 1993, and fewer than 200 in June 1993. It seemed the president and First Lady had successfully established a shield to protect their daughter from the press. And Chelsea was happy about it. When her father offered to bring her and some of her friends to Tokyo in the summer of 1993, while he was attending a summit, Chelsea declined. "She didn't want to be a big object of press interest," President Clinton confirmed.[13]

While living in the White House, Chelsea went to Sidwell Friends School, an elite Washington, DC, private school that has educated numerous children of presidents, including Sasha and Malia Obama, Archibald Roosevelt, and Tricia Nixon. The Clintons' choice of school for their daughter was somewhat controversial at the time. Chelsea had attended public school in Arkansas, and there was speculation over whether she would continue to do so in Washington, DC. The DC public schools were struggling at the time—students in the DC schools tended to score poorly on national tests, and an audit done by the American Association of School Administrators stated that the DC schools were unstable and mismanaged, with many incompetent teachers and administrators.

At the time, much of the same could be said about Arkansas public schools, whose students tended to do poorly on national tests. Yet Chelsea had performed well in Arkansas, despite a public education. Many wondered, therefore, whether Bill and Hillary Clinton would choose to make a political statement about their support of the public education system by sending Chelsea to a DC public school. R. David Hall, the president of the Washington, DC, Board of Education, stated shortly after Clinton was elected that if the Clintons sent Chelsea to public school, "It would certainly be a signal, not to just the District public schools, but to public schools across the nation that have been under fire … that the attempt to destroy public education is over."[14]

Ultimately, the Clintons settled on the elite Sidwell Friends School, and the controversy died down. As Ellen Shearer, public affairs director for the American Federation of Teachers, stated, "Where Chelsea goes to school is not as important as where Bill Clinton takes American education."[15] It seems many agreed.

Chelsea thrived at Sidwell Friends. She was a National Merit Scholar, and in her off time she continued to study dance at the Washington School of Ballet. In some ways, it wasn't much different from life in Arkansas—she still had dinner with her parents every night. "There was much about my life that also was normal," Chelsea remembers of that time. She remembers teaching her parents how to use cell phones and how to text. And she remembers their dinnertime debates continuing, covering current events and contentious political issues. "It taught me that not only was it okay to have an opinion and a point of view … it was expected," Chelsea says.[16]

Indeed, those lessons would serve Chelsea well after she left the White House and moved on to pursue higher education at Stanford University.

CHAPTER TWO

College and Graduate Years

W hen it came time for Chelsea Clinton to think about college, her father was in his second term as president. All eyes were on where the First Daughter would decide to attend school. Then, just months into her first term at college, Chelsea was thrust even more into the spotlight by a scandal that rocked her father's presidency.

Leaving for College

Chelsea had spent her teenage years growing up in the White House, and while she was largely shielded from the media by her protective parents, she was always the

Chelsea graduated from Stanford University in 2001.

object of public interest. As the first child to grow up in the White House since Amy Carter, she endured the American public's curiosity. What was her life like in the White House? What did she like to do? Would she be a rebellious teenager?

As it turned out, Chelsea was a relatively level-headed teen who didn't do much to attract public attention. She attended Sidwell Friends School, where she earned top marks, and she danced ballet. She was close to both of her parents and lived a relatively quiet, normal life for a young woman in the spotlight.

As Chelsea approached her high school graduation, she did what every college-bound teen does—she toured college campuses. With her strong academic performance, her status as a National Merit semifinalist, and her Clinton pedigree, Chelsea had her pick of universities. She reportedly considered Harvard, Yale (where both of her parents attended law school), Brown, Northwestern, Stanford, Wellesley (Hillary Clinton's **alma mater**), and Georgetown University (Bill Clinton's alma mater).

At the time, Chelsea was interested in pursuing a career in medicine—specifically, cardiology—and she ultimately chose Stanford University in Palo Alto, California, just south of San Francisco. Hillary Clinton reportedly said her stomach was in knots at the idea of Chelsea being 3,000 miles (4,800 kilometers) away from her, but she stated publicly, "I'm just grateful that this day has come. I think she wanted to branch out and be

Chelsea attended freshman orientation at Stanford with little fanfare.

her own person, make her own mark in the world." Bill
Clinton was calm about the decision, stating, "Planes run
out there and phones work out there. Email works out
there, so we'll be all right."[1]

Stanford University was delighted the welcome
Chelsea. She was one of only 2,604 applicants admitted
to the prestigious university—out of a total of 16,844
applications received that year. The university made a

Attending College with a Security Detail

Fellow Stanford classmates report that the Secret Service tried to keep as low a profile as possible, to allow Chelsea as much freedom as they could while she was at college. They dressed in casual clothes instead of suits. Fellow students reported that the only way they knew the agents were Secret Service agents was that they wore earpieces and obviously had weapons underneath their clothing. The Secret Service attended any party that Chelsea did, but they reportedly would converse with her fellow students, and they would look the other way if they saw other students engaging in questionable activities like underage drinking. Their sole purpose was to protect Chelsea—not to police the activities of other students—and they stuck to that purpose.

The Secret Service took over a room wherever Chelsea was staying—in a dorm or in a shared house. They kept a low profile and were friendly with other dorm-mates and housemates. At the request of some students, they even put on a presentation about the career path to becoming a Secret Service agent and what their jobs were like.

Fellow students report that Chelsea's room window had bulletproof glass installed and that she reportedly carried a small panic button, but other than that and the fact that she had a couple of casually dressed, friendly guys in her general vicinity at all times, she was just like any other college student at Stanford.

single brief statement about their famous new freshman: "Because she will be, from our point of view and in every way possible, a regular Stanford student, we now will refrain from any further comment."[2]

It was exactly the kind of quiet, normal experience Chelsea was looking for—except, of course, that she had a Secret Service detail.

One surprising challenge Chelsea reportedly ran into was finding a roommate—not because the White House didn't approve her potential roommates, but because several parents of other Stanford students didn't want their children rooming with such a high-profile individual as Chelsea Clinton! Stanford University uses a computer system to pair up first-year roommates, and not only did the White House have to approve the computer's pick, but the roommate's parents had to agree that their child could room with the president's daughter.

Fellow students described their fellow classmate as "always really nice and super down to earth" and "always very pleasant." One student remembered that at the departmental graduation ceremony, a metal detector was installed for all attendees to go through, since Chelsea and her parents were there. The student remembered, "As graduates' parents, grandparents, etc., lined up and filed through the metal detector, Chelsea and her mom were there standing by the metal detector and apologizing for the hassle and for distracting from their loved one's big day. I always thought that was classy."[3]

Weathering Scandal

As much as Chelsea wanted to avoid public attention, arriving at Stanford on her first day in an unassuming gray T-shirt, white pants, and tennis shoes, it wasn't long before she was again the subject of intense media scrutiny—and for nothing she herself had done.

As Chelsea was beginning her studies at Stanford in the fall of 1997, a woman not much older than her, Monica Lewinsky, began talking to a coworker, and what transpired rocked the nation.

Lewinsky was a young White House intern who engaged in an affair with President Bill Clinton from late 1995 to early 1997. Clinton administration officials had relocated Lewinsky to a position in the Pentagon in 1996, when they recognized the possibility of an improper relationship between the president and the young intern. But Lewinsky and Clinton's encounters continued until March 1997.

At the Department of Defense, Lewinsky became friends with an older coworker, Linda Tripp, and told her about the affair. Tripp began to secretly record her conversations with Lewinsky about the affair, and she also encouraged Lewinsky to keep the gifts Clinton had given her and, most damningly, not to clean a blue dress that had the president's DNA on it—proof of an intimate relationship between Lewinsky and Clinton.

The story began to leak in the fall of 1997, just as Chelsea was starting her studies at Stanford. Linda

Tripp's literary agent began to suggest to reporters that taped conversations existed that would confirm the affair. The scandal got uglier when Lewinsky perjured herself by stating in an **affidavit** that she'd had no physical relationship with Clinton, and it exploded when Tripp turned the taped conversations over to Independent Counsel Kenneth Starr. Starr was investigating Clinton's connection to the Whitewater scandal.

The full story broke in the media in late January 1998. In a press conference on January 26, 1998, Clinton stated emphatically, "I want you to listen to me. I'm going to say this again: I did not have sexual relations with that woman, Miss Lewinsky."[4]

The story dominated the headlines for the rest of 1998, particularly in the summer, when Lewinsky testified to a grand jury about her relationship with the president and turned over the blue dress with his DNA on it as evidence. By August, the DNA evidence had been confirmed, and on August 17, 1998, Clinton finally came clean, stating during a live television address:

I did have a relationship with Miss Lewinsky that was not appropriate. In fact, it was wrong. It constituted a critical lapse in judgment and a personal failure on my part for which I am solely and completely responsible ... I know that my public comments and my silence about this matter gave a false impression. I misled people, including even my wife. I deeply regret that."[5]

Clinton's other deep regret was the embarrassment he caused Chelsea, who had to endure jeers at Stanford when her parents would appear on television or when the subject of her father's womanizing came up. (Lewinsky was not Clinton's only affair; theirs was simply the most publicized of his dalliances.)

The scandal continued when the House of Representatives voted to try Clinton in the Senate for impeachment. Clinton was ultimately acquitted and remained in office, but the events certainly tarnished his reputation.

In the face of intense scrutiny, Chelsea weathered the public mocking of her family. She remained quietly but strongly supportive of both of her parents. A famous photo taken on August 18, 1998, the day after Bill Clinton admitted to the affair and his lies about it, shows Chelsea walking across the White House lawn between her parents, holding their hands. The American public saw the image as proof that Chelsea was literally and figuratively holding her family and her parents' marriage together.

Chelsea was reportedly crushed by her father's actions. Very close with her mother, Chelsea could not simply ignore the pain that her father's now-public affair caused Hillary. At the same time, she was close to her flawed father and couldn't hate him for his weakness. She had also been raised in the political spotlight and knew what political families do in the face of scandal. They put on a stoic face and move ahead, which is exactly what Chelsea did. With her trademark poise and grace,

President Clinton (*right*), Chelsea (*center*), and Hillary (*left*) walk with their dog as they leave for Martha's Vineyard in 1998.

Chelsea showed the American public that her father's failing would not destroy their family—and it didn't. Two decades later, Bill and Hillary Clinton remain married, and Bill was a strong supporter during Hillary's 2016 campaign for the presidency.

Graduate Work

On June 17, 2001, Chelsea Clinton received her bachelor's degree in history from Stanford University.

She graduated with highest honors. Somewhere along the way, she switched her focus from medicine to history, and before graduating she completed her senior thesis on the peace process in Northern Ireland, under the tutelage of her Pulitzer Prize–winning advisor, Professor Jack Rakove. Rakove described Chelsea as "really well informed. If you talk books with her, you can be blown away by how much she knows."[6]

The Clintons were proud parents at the graduation, with Bill Clinton describing his daughter as having "her mother's character and her father's energy" and saying, "I think Hillary and I are graduating too, to a new phase in our relationship with Chelsea. We are excited about it, grateful that she still wants to spend time with us, and sure I'll be learning a lot more as we tag along in her life."[7]

Following in her father's footsteps, Chelsea left for Oxford University the fall after her Stanford graduation. Bill Clinton had studied politics at Oxford under a Rhodes Scholarship, while Chelsea was admitted on the basis of her academic record at Stanford (though her famous name likely didn't hurt her chances for admission, either). She planned to study for a master's degree in a two-year international relations program.

Just as she had at Stanford, Chelsea made friends at Oxford due in part to her poise, intelligence, and friendliness. However, her initial entry to life at Oxford wasn't entirely smooth. She got to Oxford just after the terrorist attacks of September 11, 2001, at a time when anti-American sentiment was running high in some circles. She was homesick, and her initial desire to make friends from different countries was overtaken by her need to connect with fellow Americans. She wrote an article for *Talk* magazine in which she said, "Every day I encounter some sort of anti-American feeling … I thought I would seek out non-Americans as friends, just for diversity's sake. Now I find that I want to be around Americans—people who I know are thinking about our country as much as I am."[8]

Chelsea was widely criticized for the article. The *Oxford Student*, a campus newspaper, accused Chelsea of using her position as the former president's daughter to publicize a pro-war viewpoint. (By this time, Bill Clinton had completed his second term as president, and George W. Bush had taken office—and declared war after the 9/11 attacks.)

However, the furor eventually died down, and Chelsea gained acceptance in Oxford and the rest of England. Away from the scrutiny of living in America, Chelsea began to step into the spotlight more frequently in England, attending plays in London's West End and visiting popular clubs and restaurants. The editor of the United Kingdom's celebrity magazine *Tatler*, Geordie Greig, said of Oxford student Chelsea, "It seems like she's breathed English air and is jumping up and down a bit and just enjoying life. … Though it is clear that she has the famous Clinton charisma, this is a place where she can breathe her own air rather than her father's air."[9]

Chelsea at a 2002 fashion show with singer Madonna (*center left*), Madonna's daughter Lourdes (*left*), and Donatella Versace (*right*)

As much as people would like to think that outside appearances don't matter, the harsh reality is that they often do—and this may have been the case for Chelsea as well. During her time at Oxford, she fell in love (with Ian Klaus, a fellow Oxford student from the San Francisco area) and underwent a makeover. Gone was the frizzy hair of her childhood, replaced with sleek, blown-straight hair and artfully applied makeup. When she sat front and center at a Versace fashion show in London, she attracted considerable notice. Jess Cartner-Morley, the fashion editor for the *Guardian*, commented, "She looked great—she's completely attractive in real life. She was a very clever sort of person for Donatella [Versace] to get for the front row. People are interested in her life, as well as just how she looks."[10]

Clinton's attractive makeover attracted much attention, but she continued to be respected for her intelligence and grace as well. One Londoner who met her on several occasions called Chelsea "absolutely charming" and said, "She's incredibly poised for her age and has got all her parents' gifts in spades."[11] Chelsea might have had a new look, but she certainly hadn't lost the personality that had gained her respect at Sidwell Friends and at Stanford.

In 2003, after completing her thesis on the global fight against AIDS, tuberculosis, and malaria, Chelsea earned her master's degree in international relations from Oxford and returned to the United States.

However, her time in the United Kingdom was not over. Chelsea earned a master's degree in public health from Columbia University in 2010, and after that she began working on international recruitment strategies for New York University. While at NYU, she began work on her PhD. However, she transferred back to Oxford in 2011 to complete her thesis and earn her doctorate in international relations. She wrote a 712-page dissertation called *The Global Fund: An Experiment in Global Governance*, which she completed in 2014, the same year she earned her PhD.

Earning degrees wasn't all Chelsea did between 1997 and 2014. Chelsea also worked and served on several boards and foundations. As she did, she began to emerge even more into the public eye.

CHAPTER THREE

Entering the Public Eye

There has never been a time when Chelsea Clinton *wasn't* in the public eye. She was born into the Governor's Mansion in Arkansas, and she moved to the White House just before she turned thirteen. Despite her parents' attempts to shield her from the spotlight, Chelsea was thrust further into the public eye when the scandal of her father's affair with a White House intern and his subsequent perjury emerged.

As she grew up, the poised young girl who had avoided the spotlight began to step more into the public eye, particularly after she graduated from Stanford and went to Oxford. And as the years have passed, she has continued to become a more prominent face in the public.

Chelsea was honored by *Variety* at the Power of Women: New York event in 2017.

Entering the Working World

Chelsea began to step more into the public eye while living in England and attending Oxford. Her physical transformation caught the eye of the press, and Chelsea seemed more comfortable appearing at public events and being covered by the media. By the time she finished her master's degree at Oxford, she was comfortable stepping out into the working world for the first step in her career.

In 2003, when she returned to the United States, she took a job with the consulting firm McKinsey and Company. She reportedly started with a six-figure salary and worked in financial-services consulting, advising health-care and pharmaceutical businesses. Just as she had been at Stanford and Oxford, Chelsea was respected and liked at McKinsey and Company, with a colleague describing her as "very impressive, very poised."[1] Other colleagues at McKinsey and Company and at her next job, at Avenue Capital, described Chelsea as someone who "came early, stayed late, showed sound judgment, and asked no special favors."[2]

After spending three years at McKinsey and Company, Chelsea moved to Avenue Capital, a **hedge fund**, where she worked as an analyst. That career move was slightly controversial, given that Avenue Capital was cofounded by billionaire Marc Lasry, a major donor to Hillary Clinton's Senate reelection campaign. The sticky scenario grew stickier as the years went on. When Chelsea joined Avenue Capital, all that was known was that Lasry had donated to many Democratic campaigns, including Hillary Clinton's. But when Hillary hit the campaign trail in 2016, she made regulating hedge funds a big part of her campaign, suggesting that hedge fund managers were responsible, in part, for the 2008 financial crisis and might be responsible for another financial crisis in the future. By then, however, Chelsea had long since left Avenue Capital.

Moving from Jobs to Career

While Chelsea generally enjoyed her work at McKinsey and Company and at Avenue Capital, she admitted years later that it wasn't really her passion. At *Fortune*'s Most Powerful Women Summit in Washington in 2013, Chelsea told Pattie Sellers that she hadn't exactly had a clear career path in mind when she finished her master's degree.

> *I think you give me too much credit for having had a clear crystal ball in my early twenties ... I wish that I had had one galvanizing ambition that I could reverse engineer my life toward ... I tried very hard to care about things that were different than what my parents cared about, because who wants to grow up and feel like it was all just so predestined?*[3]

Financial consulting and hedge fund jobs typically pay well, but Chelsea decided money wasn't what she was looking for. "I didn't fundamentally care about money as a measure of success in my life," she said at the Most Powerful Women Summit.[4]

Chelsea with her husband, Marc Mezvinsky, in 2011

Instead, she took a long, hard look at those around her. By that point, she had broken up with Ian Klaus and was living with Marc Mezvinsky, a childhood friend and fellow Stanford and Oxford alumnus. Like Chelsea, Marc was working at a hedge fund. Chelsea remembers, "[Marc] loved what he did and the fund he was working at, and I thought, 'Wow, I need to figure out what I'm going to love as much.'"[5]

Chelsea went back to school, earning her master's degree in public health from Columbia in 2010, and she started teaching at Columbia in 2012. Also in 2010, Chelsea began work on her PhD at NYU, and she also began her term as assistant vice **provost** for NYU's Global Network University.

In this time of finding her passion, Chelsea kept busy with her studies and associated work. But what Chelsea ultimately decided she would love was working at the Clinton Foundation.

Moving from Career to Passion

The Clinton Foundation is a humanitarian nonprofit group that began as the William J. Clinton Foundation in 1997. It later became the Bill, Hillary and Chelsea Clinton Foundation, and now it is simply called the Clinton Foundation.

The Clinton Foundation's mission is to "strengthen the capacity of people in the United States and throughout the world to meet the challenges of global interdependence."[6] Chelsea joined the foundation in 2011, working on fundraising and taking a seat on the Board of Directors. As part of her work, Chelsea delivered speeches on behalf of the foundation, which brought in substantial income. Two years later, in 2013, Chelsea became vice chair of the Clinton Foundation's Board of Directors.

Much of the Clinton Foundation's work concerns global health. Given Chelsea's degrees in international relations and public health and her past interest in becoming a doctor, taking an active role in the organization was a natural fit. She doesn't discount the part her own family's history played in her decision to join the foundation, though. "I hope my parents live forever, I am deeply biased toward both of them, I love them completely, but I'm not impervious to the fact that my father had a very serious heart surgery almost nine years ago," Chelsea said in 2013.[7] Because of her belief in the foundation's mission, Chelsea wanted to ensure that when anything happens to her parents, the foundation will continue to operate.

Many humanitarian nonprofits distribute grant money to programs they wish to support, but the Clinton Foundation operates a bit differently—it funds its own programs. One such program was the Clinton HIV/AIDS Initiative, which has since spun off into its own nonprofit called the Clinton Health Access Initiative (CHAI). The initiative focuses on improving treatment of HIV and AIDS for people in low-income and middle-income countries.

On a related note, CHAI also provides antimalarial drugs in Africa and other places where malaria is a persistent problem. It also works in the area of maternal health in low- and middle-income countries. In addition to being vice chair of the board for the Clinton Foundation, Chelsea sits on the board of CHAI.

The bulk of the Clinton Foundation's expenditures go to funding CHAI. To be specific, in 2014, 57 percent of the Clinton Foundation's expenses were for running CHAI. CHAI has a big donor, though, in another well-known family. The Gates Foundation, run by cofounder of Microsoft Bill Gates and his wife, Melinda, contributed more than $60 million to CHAI in 2015.

The Clinton Foundation doesn't only address issues of global health, though. In 2006, the foundation

Chelsea addresses an audience on behalf of the Clinton Global Initiative in 2014.

spawned the Clinton Climate Initiative (CCI), which aims to fight climate change. In 2014, CCI was the Clinton Foundation's second-largest program, in terms of expenditures. The initiative has programs to prevent deforestation and rehabilitate forests, as well as to develop clean energy and aid islands that are threatened by rising oceans and other effects of climate change. One of the largest donors in 2014 to the global initiative CCI was the government of Norway.

The Clinton Foundation's third-largest program in terms of expenditures, as of 2014, was overseeing the Clinton Presidential Center in Arkansas, which houses a museum, archives, educational programs, and a school of public service work.

Another substantial arm of the Clinton Foundation is the Clinton Giustra Enterprise Partnership (CGEP), which works to stem poverty by supporting entrepreneurs who address gaps in the supply-and-distribution chains in developing countries and create employment opportunities for individuals that will inspire social impact and financial return. This is a fancy way of saying that CGEP trains people to work so that they can work themselves out of the cycle of poverty.

Another arm of the foundation was the Clinton Global Initiative (CGI), which was designed to focus on global problems. The Clinton Foundation ended most of the CGI program in 2017, but one part—CGI University—will remain. CGI U introduces the efforts of CGI to college and university students, as well as youth organizations. Although CGI has been disbanded, the fundamental ideas still exist, and the CGI U program will continue to introduce those ideas to students.

The Clinton Foundation has a number of other smaller programs and initiatives as well:

The Clinton Development Initiative targets the causes of poverty in Africa and aims to help promote sustainable economic growth.

The Alliance for a Healthier Generation is part of a partnership with the American Heart Association, and it aims to significantly decrease the problem of childhood obesity and teach children to develop healthy habits.

The Clinton Health Matters Initiative builds off of the Alliance for a Healthier Generation to help improve the health of Americans.

The No Ceilings Project studies data on the progress of females worldwide since 1995.

The Clinton Foundation in Haiti empowers females in Haiti, supports small businesses, and encourages economic growth in the country to help Haiti build a prosperous future.

The Too Small to Fail program raises awareness about how activities such as talking, reading, and singing to children from birth to age five can help prepare children for success.

As vice chair of the board, Chelsea has a strong voice in all of these programs and initiatives run by the Clinton Foundation.

Moving Into Television

In 2011, Chelsea took a three-month contract with NBC as a special correspondent. She reported on feature stories for the "Making a Difference" series aired on both NBC's *Nightly News* and *Rock Center*, hosted by Brian Williams. The correspondent job reportedly developed when Chelsea met Steve Capus, the president of NBC News. Chelsea had left Avenue Capital but hadn't really started with the Clinton Foundation yet, and she was deciding what she wanted to do. She admitted to Capus that she enjoyed the stories about people making personal contributions that she had learned when she worked on her mother's 2008 bid for the Democratic presidential nomination.

"What we talked about was if she were to come on board that's the kind of thing she would be interested in doing. We knew she wasn't going to do the lead

Other Foundation Work

In addition to working for the Clinton Foundation, Chelsea serves on the board of the School of American Ballet, where a friend, Jill Kargman, described her as "a down-to-earth presence."[8] In 2011, she also joined the board of InterActive Corp (IAC), an organization that operates more than 150 internet companies, including Match.com, the Princeton Review, Tinder, and Vimeo. She is also on the boards for the Weill Cornell Medical College, Common Sense Media, the Africa Center, and travel website Expedia. She is also cochair of New York University's Of Many Institute for Multifaith Leadership, which aims to educate and inspire religious and spiritual leaders to use dialogue and service based on multiple faiths to mobilize social change.

story. But having somebody who was going to do really captivating feature assignments for the 'Making a Difference' franchise really kind of synced up," Capus said in a 2011 interview with the *New York Times*.[9]

Captivating was certainly something Chelsea could do. She has been described by nearly everyone who worked or studied with her as "poised," "charming," and any number of other synonyms. People were already wondering whether she might prove to be the first female president of the United States, given her intelligence, her political savvy, her natural charm, and her Clinton pedigree.

Chelsea participates in a panel discussion with correspondent Jim Tankersley (*right*) and actor Angus T. Jones (*left*) in 2012.

The "Making a Difference" segment featured stories of people who volunteered to improve the lives of other people in their communities. Upon accepting the assignment, Chelsea stated, "I hope telling stories through 'Making a Difference'—as in my academic work and nonprofit work—will help me to live my grandmother's adage of 'Life is not about what happens to you, but about what you do with what happens to you.'"[10]

While some raised eyebrows at the reported annual salary of $600,000 Chelsea was offered by NBC, Chelsea stated that she intended to give most of her earnings to the Clinton Foundation and to George Washington University Hospital, in memory of her grandmother's passing.

Chelsea's broadcast debut took place on December 12, 2011, when she profiled an Arkansas afterschool program, and while some praised her for her poised, easy demeanor on camera, others felt the broadcast was lackluster. A *Washington Post* writer commented that he was surprised to see "how someone can be on TV in such a prominent way and, in her big moment, display so very little charisma—none at all. Either we're spoiled by TV's unlimited population of giant personalities or this woman is one of the most boring people of her era."[11]

Chelsea did a second report in February 2012, covering a Rhode Island charter school, which a critic for the *Baltimore Sun* called a "one-dimensional, under-reported, naïve celebration of a charter school" that was "an empty-headed puff job."[12]

But Chelsea's skills as a journalist improved, as did the public's reception of her work. In mid-2012, her report on the Maya Angelou Academy, a prison education program, was described as "smart" and "moving."[13]

Whenever a person takes a large step into the public eye, there will likely be supporters and critics. In Chelsea's case, her supporters outnumbered her critics, in the eyes of NBC. The network renewed her initial three-month contract in February 2012, and Chelsea continued the assignment until August 2014.

Stepping Into Writing

In 2015, Chelsea took a step into another form of media when she published her first book. *It's Your World: Get Informed, Get Inspired and Get Going!* was published in September 2015. It's a book for middle schoolers, and Chelsea wrote it to introduce preteens to social issues that they can address to do their part in improving the world.

The Loss of a Role Model

In 2011, in the midst of career changes and a relatively new marriage, Chelsea was touched by personal loss—her beloved maternal grandmother, Dorothy Rodham, passed away. Chelsea and Dorothy had become especially close in 1993, the year the Clintons entered the White House and Chelsea's maternal grandfather died. They grew even closer in 2001, shortly after Chelsea graduated from Stanford. "My grandmother and I spent a lot of time in Washington together, and then she was diagnosed with colon cancer four days after I graduated from Stanford," Chelsea told *Vogue*. She moved into the hospital to be with her grandmother, and she says it was "the first time where we really talked about *everything*."[14]

Dorothy was tough on her granddaughter, having herself grown up in challenging circumstances. Chelsea said in 2012, "She thought that I should be doing more with my life. She felt like we have a responsibility gene in our family. And while, thankfully, she thought I was a good daughter, a good wife, and a good friend, and that I worked hard, it was starting to become time to do something more. I think she saw it as her role to challenge me in that way."[15]

But Dorothy was loving, too. She loved to get tipsy on margaritas with Chelsea's husband, Marc Mezvinsky, while designated driver Chelsea would drive the two home. She loved football, *Dancing with the Stars*, and sharing good books with her granddaughter. And when Dorothy died, she left a gaping hole in Chelsea's life—but also the lasting reminder of a woman who challenged her to be the best she could be.

Chelsea's goal was to empower middle schoolers to look at problems including global warming, poverty, cancer, gender inequality, and obesity. The book provides a historical background for all of the problems and then talks about what individuals can do to help make a difference.

Although some critics didn't love the tone of the book, many disagreed and thought it was a well-done effort. Others, however, found it to be a mixed bag. The well-regarded *New York Times*, for example, praised the book's "wonky and sweet, impassioned and **didactic**, a little self-conscious" tone, which they found very accessible to middle schoolers.[16] The tone, they thought, was just as Chelsea might speak to a loved one. Their one complaint was that the personal stories Chelsea included were boring—they felt she could have benefited from an experienced coauthor to help smooth the dull parts. But they enjoyed the real-life examples Chelsea included of other young people making change in the world, such as the example of a Rhode Island girl who mobilized local kids to get area restaurants to donate their used cooking oil to organizations that would turn it into heating oil for underprivileged families.

The *Washington Post* found the book a bit too serious for young readers. But Chelsea disagreed, feeling that middle school students want to delve into the harder subjects. In an interview with the *Chicago Tribune*, Chelsea stated:

Chelsea at a 2015 book signing for *It's Your World*

Throughout the book, I try to strike the right balance of sensibility, information about the issues and credibility with kids. One of the things I've always been struck by when talking to kids is how curious they are about the world around them, how much more engaged they are in the world than I think adults think they are, and how much kids really do want to be treated seriously, particularly when talking about what they recognize are serious issues.[17]

Regarding the profiles of young people in the book, she said, "I hope that the stories of kids as change-makers that I share help make not only the issues a little less overwhelming but also make kids more empowered."[18] Chelsea would know. She's spent her life so far using information to help inform her actions as she works to change the world.

CHAPTER FOUR

On the Campaign Trail

C helsea Clinton has done a lot with her life in a relatively short amount of time. In her first thirty-seven years, she earned several degrees, worked in a few different jobs, settled into a prominent role as vice chair for the Clinton Foundation, and published a book. What she may be best known for thus far, though, is her prominent role in her mother's 2016 bid for the presidency.

Chelsea speaks at the Democratic National Convention in 2016.

The 2016 Primaries

In politics, things nearly always get ugly at some point, and Chelsea made one of her few public missteps when campaigning for her mother during the 2016 Democratic primaries. Hillary Clinton and Bernie Sanders were the two main Democratic candidates, and they had tried to run against each other without attacking each other much. But the two candidates disagreed on health care, and when Chelsea was campaigning for her mother in January 2016, she took a stand on Bernie Sanders's plan for universal health care.

"Senator Sanders wants to dismantle Obamacare, dismantle the CHIP program, dismantle Medicare, and dismantle private insurance. I don't want to empower Republican governors to take away Medicaid, to take away health insurance for low-income and middle-income working Americans. And I think very much that's what Senator Sanders's plan would do," she stated.[1] Although Chelsea has a master's degree in public health and is generally knowledgeable about such subjects, her statement was thought to be a mischaracterization of Sanders's plan. In response to this concern, the Clinton campaign quickly worked to clarify Chelsea's intent with the statement.

Still, politicians and the public recognized Chelsea's gaff as a simple misstatement, rather than as an outright lie. As a result, the misstep did little to harm the campaign or Chelsea's reputation. If anything, it made her a bit more human—she could make a mistake like anyone else. Chelsea had been seen by some as rather aloof and unapproachable, in part because of her restraint in the public eye. As one of her friends told *Vogue*, "She's always lived her life as if she's being watched, by which I mean she was always very well behaved and very well spoken."[2]

Chelsea's Twitter feed is rarely inflammatory. Although she speaks about her two children, Charlotte and Aidan, in public and frequently mentioned their well-being as the reason she supported her mother as president over any other candidate, she also scrupulously protects their privacy and does not generally post their pictures on social media. From the outside, Chelsea appears calm, cool, and collected in virtually all situations, the perfect protective mother and devoted daughter. So her slight misstep during the primaries gave her a touch of realness that may have been missing.

In most cases during the campaign, Chelsea was an asset. She is generally considered to be a strong public speaker. After sitting in on one of her lectures at Columbia University, *Vogue* journalist Jonathan Van Meter marveled at her ability to deliver a lecture without notes:

When she finally looks at her notes after nearly an hour, I exhale: She is human. But more than that, she is engrossing ... She has a gift for taking complicated subject matter and making it come alive. But it also has

Like her father, Chelsea is known as a strong public speaker.

to do with her lecture style: standing stock-still, speaking very slowly, her big blue eyes moving back and forth almost metronomically.[3]

That speaking style leads some to find her distant, but others find her mesmerizing. Writing for *Vogue*, Van Meter described how Chelsea could be as absent minded and forgetful as anyone, but he said that her speaking is "well worth the price of admission."[4] That was certainly an asset for the Clinton campaign, given how many voters found Hillary Clinton to be too rehearsed and almost robotic in her speaking at times. Marc Mezvinsky, Chelsea's husband, recalls telling Chelsea about her mother: "When I first saw [Hillary] campaign for the Senate twelve years ago, I said, 'Your mom speaks in fully formed paragraphs.'"[5] Mezvinsky sees that same quality in Chelsea, but in general, Chelsea's delivery has a more human touch than her mother's sometimes does.

The 2016 Presidential Race

Once Hillary won the Democratic nomination for president, it was on to battle for the presidency. It was an interesting presidential race because two daughters were major figures in the campaign, which has not been the case in past campaigns.

Hillary Clinton was going head to head with billionaire Donald Trump, a man with very little political background but a lot to say—and a lot of people who were interested in hearing it. It was a bitter battle with a lot of **mudslinging** and a lot of out-of-control media reports on both sides.

For all of her strengths as a politician, Hillary Clinton had a fatal flaw: a lot of Americans didn't like her. They thought she was dishonest (particularly about using a private email server and about her role in the **Benghazi** situation), that she had potentially used her power to try to silence some of the women with whom her husband

Chelsea's Other Half

Chelsea met her husband, Marc Mezvinsky, in 1992, when she was twelve and he was fifteen, and they both attended a Renaissance Weekend retreat. They became casual friends, and both attended Stanford, though they did not date there. They also both attended Oxford, and when Chelsea broke up with boyfriend Ian Klaus, she and Marc grew closer. Chelsea reportedly describes their romance as "like one of those bad after-school specials."[6] They became a couple in 2005, got engaged in 2009, and married in 2010.

In some ways, Mezvinsky is perhaps a surprising partner for Chelsea. He is Jewish, while Chelsea was raised by Methodist (Hillary) and Baptist (Bill) parents. Additionally, his family is no stranger to scandal—his father, Edward Mezvinsky, was convicted of fraud for embezzling more than $10 million from people in a **Ponzi scheme** and other fraudulent activities. Political families typically try to distance themselves from scandal, but the Clinton family is no stranger to scandal, so perhaps it's not such a surprise that Marc Mezvinsky's tarnished family background wasn't a deal-breaker for Chelsea.

Marc cofounded the Eaglevale Partners hedge fund, and he works as an investment banker. He and Chelsea have two children: Charlotte (born in 2014) and Aidan (born in 2016).

Chelsea and her husband, Marc, married in 2010.

had had affairs, and that she was cold and unfeeling. Whether any of that is true is inconsequential because what mattered was that was how a lot of America saw her.

For all of his strengths as a businessman, Donald Trump had a nearly fatal flaw: a lot of Americans didn't like him. They thought he was dishonest about his ties with Russia (particularly his relationship with Russian president Vladimir Putin), that he was a racist, that he was a **misogynist**, that he had very little understanding of the American political system, and that he was a **narcissist**.

In the end, for many Americans it was a matter of voting for the lesser of two evils. Which candidate did they least hate? That turned out to be Trump—at least by

A Unique First Family Dynamic

During the 2016 presidential campaign, it was noted that, regardless of which candidate would win, the result would be a unique First Family dynamic in the White House. In the early days of the United States, First Ladies tended to lead very quiet, behind-the-scenes lives. But the role became much more prominent when Eleanor Roosevelt—wife of Franklin Delano Roosevelt—was First Lady, and it generally has been ever since. Not all First Ladies have taken strong public positions on issues, but many have. Nancy Reagan was an outspoken advocate for drug-abuse prevention, for example, and Michelle Obama worked to improve healthy eating habits in children. However, Melania Trump was surprisingly quiet as she began her time as First Lady. When her husband won the election and moved into the White House, Melania remained behind in New York City to quietly raise their son, Barron. This led some to speculate that Ivanka Trump would be the *real* First Lady in the White House, even though she is the president's daughter and not his wife.

In the case of the Clintons, Chelsea has already been the First Daughter. If Hillary had won the election, Chelsea would have been First Daughter again, but she announced that she would *not* reside in the White House this time around. For the first time, the nation would have had a First Gentleman, rather than a First Lady, as Bill Clinton would have assumed the role his wife held two decades earlier.

the **electoral vote**. Hillary Clinton won the **popular vote** by about three million votes—a fact that Trump disputes.

This is where the two daughters—Ivanka Trump and Chelsea Clinton—came into play. Their presence in the campaign humanized their detested parents. Some people felt Trump couldn't be as much of a misogynist as he seemed, given Ivanka's constant presence in his campaign—someone who found women inferior certainly wouldn't put a woman in a powerful position, they felt. And Hillary couldn't possibly be as cold and unfeeling as she seemed if Chelsea was such a constant presence. A cold mother couldn't raise such a devoted daughter, people felt.

At the 2016 Democratic National Convention, First Lady Michelle Obama pointed to Chelsea as proof of Hillary's ability to lead the nation, saying:

> *I am here tonight because in this election, there is only one person ... who I believe is truly qualified to be president of the United States, and that is our friend Hillary Clinton. See, I trust Hillary to lead this country because I've seen her lifelong devotion to our nation's children—not just her own daughter, who she has raised to perfection—but every child who needs a champion.[7]*

It was a powerful statement because few could dispute it. Chelsea was living proof that her mother had done a fantastic job of leading her to adulthood. No matter how many people disliked Hillary, most did not

An Unlikely Friendship

Oddly enough, given how tense the relationship between Hillary Clinton and Donald Trump grew to be, Chelsea Clinton and Ivanka Trump are friends who have a deep mutual respect for each other. They are both working mothers to young children; until 2017, both lived in New York City; and both married Jewish men. But as the campaign grew angrier between the two candidates, Chelsea began speaking out more against Ivanka's father, Donald Trump. In April 2016, she spoke to reporters about "Mr. Trump's rhetoric of sexism and racism and Islamophobia and anti-immigrant hatred."[8] She continued to voice her distaste for Trump's policies and politics as the campaign went on. Not surprisingly, that led to a cooling off of the women's friendship, though they claim to still have strong respect for each other.

dislike Chelsea—she had thus far led an exemplary life that did not invite much criticism. Some critics felt she grew up with a **silver spoon** in her mouth and looked at life through the lens of growing up privileged. She has occasionally made public missteps, but in general her actions have been above reproach, and many citizens find her a relatively likable figure.

Indeed, Chelsea's strengths often bolster the image of her mother. CNN described Chelsea as having a "unique ability to make a personal pitch, softening and humanizing Hillary Clinton's image to that of a mother and grandmother."[9] She also spoke to what she felt were her mother's strengths, such as when she told a crowd that the next president must be "a dreamer and a doer and, I would also argue, a fighter. And I don't know anyone who combines that more effectively and powerfully than my mom."[10]

Chelsea's role in the campaign was quiet and understated, but powerful. While Ivanka Trump was a prominent person in the Trump campaign—*Politico* described her well-defined role by saying, "She [is] the polished young adult who could humanize her blustery dad"—Chelsea had a less defined role.[11]

Part of that was due to biology: during the first half of 2016, Chelsea was pregnant with her second child. (Son Aidan was born in June.) Still, during that first half of the year, Chelsea made more than a hundred campaign appearances for her mother and met with political strategists along with her parents. After Aidan's birth and time taken off to recover, Chelsea was back on the campaign trail.

In September 2016, when the presidential race was particularly fierce due to the upcoming debates and with Election Day closing in, Chelsea stepped in when her mother was sidelined by pneumonia. While for most adults pneumonia is a serious but treatable illness, it became a major problem for Hillary Clinton because the Trump team and her opponents used the illness to question her fitness for office. Was she healthy enough to take on the office of the presidency? Was pneumonia a sign of her failing health?

Hillary needed to continue to make a strong statement even while sidelined by illness, and so her husband and daughter stepped in and campaigned for her while she recovered. According to the *Washington Times*, political analysts speculated that it was actually a wise move for the Clinton campaign because both Bill and Chelsea Clinton had higher favorability ratings with voters than Hillary did. William Chafe, a Duke University historian who has followed the Clintons for decades, commented that "Chelsea is a more neutral figure [than her mother], an attractive personality and a young mother."[12]

Behind the scenes, too, Chelsea has always been a trusted advisor to Hillary. Hillary reportedly considered all of Chelsea's feedback and suggestions during her 2016 campaign. Chelsea also served as a pillar of strength and support for her mother during the grueling campaign. Huma Abedin, vice chair for Hillary Clinton's 2016 presidential campaign, said during the campaign, "The moment in Hillary's life when she is happiest is when there's a call from Chelsea. Even if we are in the middle of a horrible, *horrible* meeting, she'll answer the phone and say, "HIIII, CHELSEA!" It's just the best sound."[13]

Chelsea was also there for her mother when the campaign ended with Hillary's defeat. On Election Day, she posted on social media: "One of the greatest honors of my life was voting for you today mom. As always, I am beyond proud of you."[14] And after the election defeat, she echoed her mother's sentiments, saying, "Everything we believed before the election, we still believe. Everything we worked so hard for, we have to continue to work hard for … Use [your] emotions to engage and organize and advocate to protect and advance what you think matters most. Whether that's combatting climate change, or protecting women's rights, fighting against gun violence, or advocating for **LGBTQ** equality."[15]

Typical Chelsea—determined and looking ahead to how she can inspire others to make a difference.

CHAPTER FIVE

Activism

One of Chelsea Clinton's big passions is working toward positive change and inspiring others to do the same. She wrote her book *It's Your World: Get Informed, Get Inspired and Get Going!* to inspire middle schoolers to find ways to work toward making positive changes on issues that are important to them. And she continues to work on projects that are important to her.

Supporting the Millennial Generation and Beyond

Millennials get a bad rap by many in the older generations. People in previous generations characterize millennials as lazy, entitled people who don't want to work for what they're given, and often that generalization extends to the generation following millennials, too. But

Chelsea Clinton in 2015

Chelsea doesn't see that characterization as true. Far from it, in fact. In an interview with the *Chicago Tribune* when her book was released, Chelsea said:

> *I meet kids who are, at a minimum, curious about the world around them, and many who are already engaged in making a difference in areas they care about ... If you think about the millennial generation, it's the most participatory in terms of volunteering time since that has been measured. In the last year, in studies done by Pew [Research] and others, more than half of the millennial participants surveyed volunteered at least once, either through their work or their college or community college or church. So I think young people are more engaged than often they're given credit for.*[1]

Chelsea's support of millennials may not be particularly surprising, since she just barely missed the cutoff herself. Millennials are normally considered to be people born between about 1982 and the year 2000, and Chelsea was born just two years earlier.

Supporting Women

Another cause that has been near and dear to Chelsea's heart is women's rights. This, too, is not overly surprising, given the strong role model her mother has been. Hillary Clinton spent much of her early career as a lawyer fighting for the rights of women and children, and she continued to make that a platform as she moved into politics. Chelsea, it seems, has followed in her mother's footsteps there.

In her first book, Chelsea included a number of scenarios from her own life growing up, and one was a situation in which a boy sat on her in first grade and wouldn't get off, even after Chelsea told him to. The teacher's response to Chelsea was, "Boys will be boys," which stunned Chelsea, even at age six. Recalling the incident, Chelsea says, "That was such a shock to my system, because I'd never been told that I couldn't do something because I was a girl. I had never been told that I should expect to not be treated equal to the boys in my neighborhood, the boys at church, the boys in my classroom."[2]

As a mother to a young daughter now, Chelsea reflects on that long-ago situation and how it informs her actions today:

I care even more intensely about all these issues than I did when I first started working on [my book]. I care with even sharper edges about issues relating to girls and women, because I hope that Charlotte never has to have a shock that I did when I realized all these different ways in which girls and women were treated differently.[3]

As part of her work on women's rights issues, Chelsea is heavily involved in the Clinton Foundation's No Ceilings: The Full Participation Project. This initiative has the goal of advancing the full participation of females

Chelsea and her husband, Marc, with their newborn daughter in 2014

in society, worldwide. The initiative points to evidence that both economic prosperity and global security can be enhanced by realizing gender equality.

More specifically, the idea behind the initiative is that when women more fully participate in the labor force and are encouraged to explore entrepreneurship opportunities, economies see an increase in their gross domestic product (GDP) and a decrease in their poverty rates. However, to get women to be able to enjoy full participation in the labor force, they must be healthy and educated. Thus, the initiative explores the gaps in equality between females and males and strives to close those gaps, particularly in the areas of health, education, and labor/entrepreneurship. Another piece of the initiative shines a light on cultural acceptance of gender-based violence—women who are abused are at an obvious disadvantage when it comes to their ability to fully participate in their societies and economies.

No Ceilings: The Full Participation Project is a worldwide effort because Chelsea and other members of the Clinton Foundation recognize that gender inequality isn't a localized problem—it affects women around the world. In a March 2016 essay for the website Mogul, Chelsea says:

> *There has never been a better time in human history to be born female. And yet, today, we know that girls and women make up the majority of the world's undereducated and uneducated and remain the world's biggest source of untapped potential. In 2016, it's still true that in no country on earth are women given equal rights and equal opportunities—to education, to health care, to equal pay for equal work—to men.*[4]

In typical balanced, polished Chelsea form, she makes reference to the gains in gender equality that have been made over the past two decades. For instance, girls are now entering elementary school at equal rates to boys, maternal mortality has been cut by nearly 50 percent, and more constitutions are protecting women's rights. But she also cites the gaps that still exist between the genders. For example, more than eight hundred women still die each day due to complications of pregnancy or childbirth. Women's participation in the labor force has slowed over the last two decades. Women are earning fewer computer science degrees today than they did thirty years ago. And in the United States, maternal mortality rates have actual risen in the past twenty-five years. "We can and must do more to change this," Chelsea writes. [5]

After citing the steps taken by a number of women to improve gender equality worldwide, Chelsea issues a call to action:

> International Women's Day shouldn't be over on March 8th—or forgotten just a week later—so let's each commit to working together to stay informed and working toward a world in which every girl and woman—no matter where she's born—has the opportunity to live up to her full potential. Our future depends on it. [6]

As much as Chelsea is a strong supporter of gender equality, she is not alone in her efforts. She works as one part of the Clinton Foundation, and when it comes to No Ceilings: The Full Participation Project, the Clinton Foundation has partnered with another powerful force in the fight for gender equality—the Gates Foundation. Melinda Gates is another strong female advocate working on a number of global issues, one of which is gender equality. The partnership between the two foundations on this particular project is not surprising.

Women's Rights Advocate ... and a Mom

As vocal as Chelsea is about women's rights and encouraging women to participate in the workforce, she has another side that humanizes her to a lot of women. She is, first and foremost, a mom, and she has the same sorts of challenges a lot of other mothers have. After having her first baby, daughter Charlotte, Chelsea took some time off work. When she returned to working full time, she found herself in the same predicament as many working mothers: How to pump breast milk for her daughter while working? In an interview with E!, she said, "I was still breastfeeding and I was pumping and I was so committed to ensuring I could keep doing that for Charlotte, and balancing those logistics was really hard … [I had to get] comfortable with pumping in airport bathrooms and kind of wherever I needed to get it done."[7]

While Chelsea undoubtedly has an easier time of it than working moms who perhaps don't have the support of a partner or don't have the financial resources Chelsea does, it's a humanizing touch to realize that Chelsea Clinton, who some think may be the first female president of the United States, struggles with the same working-mom problem as millions of other working mothers.

Supporting the LGBTQ Community

Chelsea Clinton is a staunch believer in equal rights for women, but she also believes in equality for the LGBTQ community. She has numerous friends in the community and is credited for influencing her mother to support same-sex marriage. In 2014, she called issues of LGBTQ rights "the unfinished business of the twenty-first century."[8]

At a 2014 Human Rights Campaign conference, Chelsea spoke about bullying of gay youth, saying, "Changing laws and changing the political dialogue, while necessary, is insufficient to ensure that bullying stops; to ensure that every young person is supported by their parents and their teachers as they question who they are and they discover who they are, regardless of their sexuality."[9] That belief has continued as Chelsea has welcomed her own children into the world and thought about their futures. She told Ellen DeGeneres in 2015, "I am just so proud that our country is the country that I want my daughter to grow up in so she can marry whoever she wants to marry."[10]

While she supports the LGBTQ community, Chelsea openly admits that there are limits to her knowledge of the subject, given that she is a heterosexual woman. At a forum in New York City during the 2016 campaign season, a transgender man asked Chelsea how people could help Hillary Clinton (if she were elected president) bring the conversation about transgender and reproductive issues to life. Chelsea responded, "I would

CLINTON GLOBAL INITIATIVE

In this 2014 speech, Chelsea famously referred to LGBTQ issues as "the unfinished business of the twenty-first century."

say you know how best to do that … I'm willing to own that I didn't start thinking about this until a few years ago, when I had a friend who was navigating similar issues. So I don't have twenty years of thinking about it."[11]

The answer frustrated some, who found it vague. However, others appreciated Chelsea's candor in admitting that it's not a question she can fully answer— or at least not as well as someone who has been living it for two decades. She has, however, been strongly committed to the issue of marriage equality since 2010, when she married her husband, whom she calls her best friend: "It just crystallized so fundamentally to me that everyone should be allowed to marry their best friend …

So I joined the equal marriage fight in New York, and we got equal marriage in New York in 2011."[12]

LGBTQ rights were at the forefront of the 2016 election for one very big reason: Donald Trump's running mate for vice president, Mike Pence, was a known opponent to gay rights during his time as a member of Congress and governor of Indiana, and he reportedly supported **conversion therapy**, an incredibly controversial practice that has been rejected by the American Medical Association and the American Psychological Association.

Pence states that he does not support conversion therapy, but a statement on the website for his 2000 congressional campaign said, "Federal dollars [should] no longer [be] given to organizations that celebrate and encourage the types of behaviors that facilitate the spreading of the HIV virus. Resources should be directed toward those institutions which provide assistance to those seeking to change their sexual behavior."[13] Combined with his stated opposition to same-sex marriage and to laws that protect gay people from discrimination, this statement led the public to believe that "institutions which provide assistance to those seeking to change their sexual behavior" likely referred to treatment centers using conversion-therapy tactics.

Given that the United States Supreme Court had recently ruled for marriage equality and that the Obama administration had supported gay rights, it is not surprising that LGBTQ advocates came out in full force against vice presidential candidate Mike Pence—and by extension, presidential candidate Donald Trump, whose platform was not particularly friendly to the rights of the LGBTQ community. The Republican Party faced numerous questions about whether they supported conversion therapy, and they were somewhat vague in their responses, leading people to wonder what their true stand on it was.

Perhaps in response to the Republicans and perhaps simply because of her belief system, Hillary Clinton came out strongly supportive of LGBTQ rights issues, as did Chelsea. At a July 2016 event for LGBTQ Democratic National Convention delegates, Chelsea was decidedly vocal in her opinions.

I think what I found most offensive really has to be, as a mom, the open embrace of conversion therapy in the Republican Party platform. In other words, child abuse … When I think about the world that I hope for my children, when I hope that they can be safe and secure and loved and supported and be whomever they want to be and whomever they feel called to be with, whomever they want to love in their lives, that vision is at risk given what Trump and Pence are currently campaigning on.[14]

Politicians are notorious for speaking in circles and not really saying what's on their mind (lest they offend or upset any potential voters), but Chelsea was quite vocal in her opposition. However, she didn't simply criticize the Trump/Pence agenda; she went on to talk about her mother's plans for advancing LGBTQ rights. If elected, Hillary would sign the Equality Act into law, sign legislation **barring** conversion therapy nationwide (several states have state laws barring it already), assist LGBTQ youth in obtaining services and support as necessary, and restore the military records of servicepersons who had previously been discharged from the military because of their sexual orientation. Whether such campaign promises would have come to fruition is anyone's guess, but that was the platform Hillary ran on—and Chelsea strongly supported.

In a full-circle moment, Chelsea channeled her mother when she introduced the presidential nominee at the Democratic National Convention in 2016, saying that her mother "knows that LGBT rights are human rights." It harkened back to Hillary's famous speech at the United Nations Fourth World Conference on Women, held in Beijing in 1995, where the then-First Lady stated, "Women's rights are human rights."[15] Women's rights are certainly in the forefront of Chelsea's consciousness, but so are LGBTQ rights.

Supporting Animal Rights

One other area Chelsea Clinton is passionate about is a bit of a surprising departure from her more common areas of activism. Chelsea supports women's rights,

LGBTQ rights, children's empowerment, and …
elephant rights?

Elephant rights indeed. Chelsea has a little-known
passion for elephants, and she is a committed advocate for
stopping the practice of **poaching**. As part of the Clinton
Global Initiative, Chelsea and other Clinton Foundation
members worked with a number of partners, including
the Wildlife Conservation Society, the World Wildlife
Fund, the Nature Conservancy, and several African
governments, to target the chief drivers of the poaching
industry. Those drivers include the suppliers (the poachers
themselves) and those who create the demand (those
willing to buy the ivory gathered by poachers).

The $80 million initiative was designed with the
hope of eventually stopping the ivory poaching trade
altogether. The money was earmarked for officials to hire
and train more than three thousand park rangers at fifty
sites in Africa, to fund the use of sniffer-dog teams along
the common smuggling routes, and to train legal officials
on prosecuting international **trafficking** gangs, among
other efforts.

Chelsea's devotion to elephants reportedly came
about in 1997, when she took a trip to Tanzania with her
mother. Both women developed a love for the animals,
and during the Clinton administration, President Bill
Clinton opposed the ivory trade. Chelsea and her parents
have since made several return trips to Africa, in part for
their work on the initiative to end elephant poaching.

The implications of poaching aren't simply the destruction of an animal species. Indeed, that is an issue—it's reported poachers have claimed the lives of at least 110,000 elephants in the past ten years, and some say nearly 100,000 were killed between 2010 and 2012 alone. Either way, the trend is pushing elephants closer to extinction. However, another issue is that the illegal ivory trade indirectly helps to fund terrorist groups, as well as **syndicates** that are involved in human, drug, and weapons trafficking. An investigative journalist for *National Geographic* hid GPS trackers in fake elephant tusks and was able to trace their path through the poaching network in Africa and beyond. He found that ultimately, the ivory (fake, in this case, of course) was used to fund the African terrorist group Lord's Resistance Army; the brutal Sudanese army (led by the Sudanese president, who has been indicted on charges of genocide, war crimes, and crimes against humanity for his role in the deaths of more than three hundred thousand innocent citizens); al-Shabaab (a Somali terrorist group); ISIS; and other terrorist groups.

Chelsea's goal in working to end poaching of elephants isn't only to save an animal species she loves from a brutal, unnecessary death; it's also to try to stop a funding stream from reaching terrorist groups. The illegal ivory trade reportedly yields $7 billion to $10 billion in annual revenue, with ivory tusks fetching about $1,000 per pound in China.

Chelsea and her mother on a 1997 safari in Tanzania

Not surprisingly, poachers, terrorist groups, and others who benefit from the illegal ivory trade aren't anxious to see it stopped. But Chelsea is determined. "My mom and I both realized independently that we were facing a real poaching crisis," Chelsea said in a 2015 speech given in Samburu, Kenya. "We knew we had to do something."[16]

As usual, Chelsea took action where she saw a need. Whether it's women's rights, LGBTQ rights, or animal rights, Chelsea's activism is always forward-focused and thoughtful.

CHAPTER SIX

Recognition and Future Plans

Chelsea Clinton has accomplished much in less than four decades on this earth, but she still has many more years to come. One beauty of being young is that she still has decades in which to continue her work on women's issues, LGBTQ issues, and other areas of focus that interest her. At present time, the future for Chelsea involves a new book and the ever-present speculation about whether she will enter politics.

Chelsea at a stop on her 2017 book tour for *It's Your World*

A Second Book

Although Chelsea Clinton's first book received mixed reviews from critics, she announced in March 2017 that she would be publishing a second book. Instead of writing for a middle-school audience, this time Chelsea would gear the book toward younger children. She said the new book would be called *She Persisted* and that it would profile thirteen women who pursued their goals despite facing strong opposition—and persisted.

The title is a reference to a statement made by Senate Majority Leader Mitch McConnell in early 2017. When President Trump announced his pick of Senator Jeff Sessions for attorney general, many people—particularly Democrats—were appalled. Sessions has a negative track record on racial and disability issues from his time as a United States attorney in Alabama and as a senator. Sessions reportedly made numerous racist remarks during his tenure in Alabama, as well as making disparaging remarks about students with disabilities.

As in almost any situation of this type, there are those who believe Sessions is a racist and those who think the allegations are false. But when it came time for Sessions's Senate confirmation hearing for the position of attorney general, Senator Elizabeth Warren spoke up against him. As part of her speech, she attempted to read a letter written in 1986 by Coretta Scott King (Martin Luther King Jr.'s widow) about Sessions's record on civil rights issues. She was interrupted by the Senate chair and then ordered by McConnell to stop her speech. It is extremely unusual for any member of the Senate to be silenced, and women felt Warren's silencing particularly keenly, given that for generations, they felt themselves silenced on important matters.

McConnell explained how Warren "persisted" even though she was warned. For many women, it sounded like McConnell was scolding an errant child, not addressing a colleague with the respect due to an esteemed senator. The statement became a battle cry for women's rights—with women celebrating examples of women who "persisted."

Chelsea took up that cry and wrote her book, which features stories of such women as Helen Keller; Oprah Winfrey; abolitionist Harriet Tubman; pioneering journalist Nellie Bly; Maria Tallchief, the first Native American to hold the title of prima ballerina in the United States; pioneer of the civil rights movement Claudette Colvin; consumer activist and early supporter of labor unions Clara Lemlich; Ruby Bridges, the first African American student to desegregate an all-white school during the New Orleans desegregation crisis; Margaret Chase Smith, the first woman to serve in both houses of Congress; first American female in space Sally Ride; Florence Griffith Joyner, the fastest female track athlete of all time; and Sonia Sotomayor, the first Latina justice on the Supreme Court. It was announced that the book would also feature the story of one more inspiring woman, who many assumed would be Hillary Rodham Clinton (though at the time of this writing, it has not been revealed). According to Chelsea via Twitter, the book features girls and women who wouldn't take no for an answer.

Upon announcing the book's impending publication, Chelsea explained:

> *I wrote this book for everyone who's ever wanted to speak up but has been told to quiet down, for everyone who's ever been made to feel less than. The 13 women in* She Persisted *all overcame adversity to help shape our country—sometimes through speaking out, sometimes by staying seated, sometimes by captivating an audience. With this book, I want to send a message to young readers around the country—and the world—that persistence is power.*[1]

No doubt the book will inspire young readers, just as the women profiled in the book inspired its author.

A Run for Office

The eternal question is whether Chelsea will run for president someday, or if not for president, perhaps for some other public office. She's a Clinton, after all, and the name Clinton is rather synonymous with politics, just as the name Kennedy is. Chelsea has proven herself knowledgeable about politics and comfortable in that world, particularly with her active participation in her mother's presidential campaign.

Although Chelsea hasn't said definitively one way or the other whether she'll enter politics, many think she's being groomed to run for Congress or the Senate, and perhaps eventually for the presidency. Media outlets such as the *Washington Post* point to Chelsea's Twitter feed as proof that she's getting more involved in politics by the day—Chelsea questions President Trump and his administration regularly via the Twitter platform. As the *Post* stated in a February 2017 article, "[Chelsea has] never really driven a political message. Until now. In recent days, we've noticed a different Chelsea Clinton— one more than willing to speak out, often a bit bluntly. And she's speaking out specifically against President Trump, using his preferred medium: Twitter."[2]

A Twitter feed alone doesn't provide proof of Chelsea's future intentions, but no one would be surprised if she did decide to enter the political arena. As one former aide to Hillary Clinton said, "[Chelsea has] never denied that she has an interest in running for office, and that leads me to believe that one day she will. And she'd probably be successful."[3] Chelsea herself also told Sky News in 2015, "Absolutely, I'd consider [running for office] one day. Right now I live in a city and a state and a country where I support my elected officials. But if that were to change and if at the same time I were to think that other people could be better advocates for [the issues I care about], then I'd have to ask and answer that question."[4]

A Twitter War

Donald Trump's presidency marks a shift in presidential communications to the nation. With presidents past, citizens have relied on televised press conferences, addresses to the nation, and press releases circulated through media outlets to hear from the president. President Obama did use social media to some extent, but not extensively. President Trump, however, delights in Twitter as a means to talk directly to the American public. He regularly tweets about whatever is on his mind. While some have responded positively to his tweets, others have met them with ire and frustration.

Chelsea Clinton, who previously used Twitter primarily to praise her mother during the campaign, to praise the Obamas, or to announce major events like the birth of her children, began taking to Twitter regularly after the 2016 election to express her disagreement with the president and his cabinet. In February 2017, Chelsea scolded Trump's counselor Kellyanne Conway for citing a terrorist attack in Bowling Green, Kentucky, that never actually happened. She has attacked Trump's ban on refugees multiple times. She has tweeted her disgust over Trump's plan to deregulate Wall Street and over Trump's reportedly incoherent speech at a Black History Month event.

Somewhat surprisingly, Trump, who has fired back on Twitter numerous times against other detractors, has mostly ignored Chelsea's Twitter commentary during the early months of his presidency, making their Twitter war rather one-sided.

Chelsea and her mother at the final rally of her mother's 2016 presidential campaign

Some feel the timing isn't right for Chelsea to enter politics—yet. When Hillary Clinton lost the 2016 election, there was a lot of animosity surrounding it. Many of her supporters were simply disappointed at the loss, but some felt Hillary had been too arrogant, too sure of her likelihood of winning, too dismissive of the voters in states that ended up voting for Trump, even when it was assumed they would vote Democratic. An aide on Hillary Clinton's presidential campaign stated, "Even if it's a year or two or three from now, I still don't think the timing would be right. I know that's not fair to [Chelsea], but nothing feels right about it. It feels too forced."[5]

Ultimately, of course, the choice is Chelsea's—and one she will no doubt consider carefully, balancing her own political ambitions with her other work and her life as a mother.

Another Child?

Many also wonder whether Chelsea and husband Marc will choose to expand their family beyond the two children they already have. The couple has not stated either way what their future plans are for family. What is known is how happy they are with their son and daughter—and what doting grandparents Bill and Hillary Clinton are.

In May 2016, while Chelsea awaited the birth of her son, Hillary told *People* magazine, "Watching Chelsea mother Charlotte is just the greatest joy. And I also occasionally feel a little bit happy that I kind of see something coming back that I maybe did or said."[6]

Chelsea admits she doesn't always take her mother's advice on parenting, but she says that for Charlotte's future, she would like to see "the same gift of imagination and kind of sense of possibility that my mom gave me."[7]

Awards and Recognition

In March 2017, *Variety* magazine, in collaboration with Lifetime Entertainment, announced that Chelsea had been selected as one of six women to be recognized as a 2017 Impact Honoree. Chelsea was selected for the award in recognition of her humanitarian work—specifically, her work on the Alliance for a Healthier Generation. This program aims to "reduce the prevalence of childhood obesity and to empower kids to develop lifelong, healthy habits."[8] The program was cofounded by the Clinton Foundation and the American Heart Association.

While the award is prestigious, it isn't the first one Chelsea has won. In 2014, *Glamour* magazine named her Woman of the Year and the Women's Champion. The magazine honored Chelsea for the No Ceilings project (an initiative of the Clinton Foundation) and also for work she has done in Africa—in particular, her work on an initiative regarding fertilizer designed to improve crop output and her work on lowering the cost of diarrhea treatments. (While diarrhea may be just a relatively common annoyance to people in the United States, in developing countries such as those in Africa, diarrhea is responsible for the deaths of hundreds of thousands of children a year.)

Chelsea jokingly promised not to talk about diarrhea when accepting the award, but she did make a serious statement on women's rights:

> *I didn't know I could care more about [women's rights] until I became a mother of a daughter. I want Charlotte to grow up to be whatever she dreams to be, wherever she dreams to be it and however she chooses to become it. And that's not the world we live in today. And so for Charlotte, for the girls up in the rafters, for girls everywhere, I'm going to continue to push forward.*[9]

Undoubtedly, there are more awards to come in Chelsea's future, as she continues to move forward with her activism and humanitarian work.

Becoming Chelsea

The Chelsea Clinton who has emerged in the past few years is a reflection of her parents—but a reflection that has increasingly taken on its own form. Those long-ago dinnertime conversations and debates with her parents taught Chelsea to think for herself, and indeed she does that. At the same time, she remains fiercely supportive of her parents and, in many ways, reflects their ideals.

For example, both Chelsea and Hillary are fierce supporters of women's rights. Another thing they share in common is that neither one excels in public speaking. Both are certainly passable at it, but neither one is particularly dynamic. This is an area where Chelsea has moved beyond and edged out her mother, though. While neither will likely ever be known as a masterful orator like Presidents Bill Clinton or Barack Obama, both can hold their own, and Chelsea is, in fact, generally considered to be a stronger speaker than Hillary. As journalist Michelle Cottle noted in the *Atlantic* in 2016, "There are no rough edges to [Chelsea]. No seams. No rambling or verbal filler. Like Hillary, Chelsea is neither an inspirational nor a motivational speaker. But her soothing aspect is strangely compelling, like that of a meditation guide or a priest."[10]

Also like her mother, Chelsea is not terribly at ease with the press. She likes to maintain control, and journalist Cottle described Chelsea as "methodical, deliberate, cautious, detail-oriented, and disciplined"—a person who "tries to keep an iron grip on her own narrative."[11] That guarded persona is something Hillary Clinton has been criticized for herself, and it seems Chelsea shares that characteristic. But Chelsea is known for being extremely caring and warm on a personal level, which isn't a quality her mother has typically been known for. When journalist Cottle was working on her story on Chelsea, she stated that two different women told her, "Chelsea is so caring and devoted … that she makes you wonder whether you are, perhaps, her only friend."[12] Whereas Hillary has struggled to shake her characterization as a generally cold, controlling person, Chelsea comes across as apprehensive around the media, but quite warm one on one. Perhaps this is the influence of both parents. Where Hillary is known to be very controlled, Bill Clinton excelled politically in part due to his charm. He was the easygoing, friendly guy who got along with nearly everyone. Chelsea, it seems, is a mix of her charming father and her more controlled mother.

Although Chelsea is devoted to her parents and generally does not seem to object to comparisons between her and her parents, she is quick to point out that she is also her own person. When reporters questioned whether she would live again at the White House if her mother won the 2016 election, Chelsea pointed out that she has a job and her family in New York and would continue living there. "My life will remain in New York," she stated.[13]

Chelsea has publicly expressed her frustration with being forever seen as an appendage to her famous parents, but at the same time she recognizes that this position has opened doors for her. While some of her achievements have been simply the product of her own hard work, other achievements have come around in part because of her famous name. For example, her assignment as a special correspondent for NBC News was undoubtedly influenced by her identity. Many people earn higher degrees in international relations and end up doing global work, but most of them don't end up being hired as a special correspondent. Her position at the Clinton Foundation was also influenced by who she is.

Chelsea walks a fine line between forging her own path and continuing down the path her parents have made. She believes in their causes and wants to work to continue them, thus her work as part of the Clinton Foundation. As Chelsea's friend from Stanford told the *Atlantic*, "When you've seen the positive impact that can come from a life of public service and the kind of difference you can make on a large scale, it's hard to move away from that."[14] At the same time, Chelsea is her own person with her own ideas. In a way, the Clinton Foundation is the perfect place for her. She has the backing of the family's fortune, but she has enough autonomy within the foundation to be able to pursue causes that interest her, such as her work on controlling elephant poaching.

Chelsea, Moving Forward

Chelsea Clinton's life has been fascinating because so much of it has been lived in the public eye. From her first appearance in the media, when she graced the front page of an Arkansas newspaper, Chelsea has been of interest to the public. When she entered the White House as a smart and somewhat awkward preteen, Americans watched her with interest. As Chelsea grew into a college student and then a graduate student, Americans watched the choices she made. She even largely won their approval. In part, she won it because of her grace and poise, but in part she won it because of how relatable she is. She had flawed parents, but she let it be known that she loved them and that she forgave them for their own missteps. She runs the same Manhattan streets that other young women do. And when Chelsea became a mother, she faced some of the same struggles other women did.

In short, Chelsea is every woman—but then, also, she's a model for what women with an eye toward activism want to be. She sees a problem, and she addresses it. She has power and privilege that many women don't have, but she appears to use them for good. She is her mother's daughter in ambition, but without the harder edges that some find distasteful in Hillary Clinton.

The future looks bright for Chelsea Clinton, the woman who seems to embody the best attributes of both of her parents—her father's charm and her mother's drive. No doubt whatever she sets her mind to, she will accomplish.

Timeline

1993

Chelsea moves into the White House and assumes the role of First Daughter.

2006

Leaves McKinsey and Company to work for Avenue Capital Group.

2001

Graduates from Stanford University and then enters Oxford University.

Chelsea Victoria Clinton is born in Little Rock, Arkansas.

1980

Graduates from Oxford University with a master's degree in international relations. Begins work as a consultant for McKinsey and Company.

2003

Graduates from high school at Sidwell Friends School and enters Stanford University.

1997

Campaigns for mother Hillary Clinton's presidential campaign.

2007–2008

2010

Graduates from Columbia University with a master's degree in public health. Begins PhD work at New York University while serving as assistant vice-provost for NYU's Global Network University. Transfers course work to Oxford University. Marries Marc Mezvinsky in Rhinebeck, New York.

2012

Begins teaching graduate classes as an adjunct professor at Columbia University.

2015

Publishes first book, *It's Your World: Get Informed, Get Inspired and Get Going!*

Welcomes second child, Aidan Clinton Mezvinsky. Campaigns for mother Hillary Clinton's presidential campaign.

2016

Welcomes first child, Charlotte Clinton Mezvinsky.

2014

Begins working for the Clinton Foundation and as a special correspondent for NBC News, reporting for the "Making a Difference" segments.

2011

SOURCE NOTES

Chapter 1

1. Amy Bingham, "Chelsea Clinton's Childhood: No Pizza, Cartoons on Weekdays," ABC News, May 7, 2012, http://abcnews.go.com/blogs/politics/2012/05/chelsea-clintons-childhood-no-pizza-cartoons-on-weekdays.

2. Hillary Clinton, *It Takes a Village* (New York: Simon and Schuster, 1996).

3. Jonathan Van Meter, "Waiting in the Wings: An Exclusive Interview with Chelsea Clinton," *Vogue*, August 13, 2012, http://www.vogue.com/article/waiting-in-the-wings-an-exclusive-interview-with-chelsea-clinton.

4. Ibid.

5. Chelsea Clinton, "Throwback Thursday: Me and My Mom, Hillary Clinton," PopSugar, August 25, 2016, https://www.popsugar.com/news/Family-Pictures-Chelsea-Hillary-Clinton-42038620.

6. Ed Pilkington, "The Joke That Should Have Sunk McCain," *Guardian*, September 1, 2008, https://www.theguardian.com/lifeandstyle/2008/sep/02/women.johnmccain.

7. Susan Baer, "Making a Private Life in a Public Family: Clintons Shield Chelsea from Spotlight," *Baltimore Sun*, July 6, 1993, http://articles.baltimoresun.com/1993-07-06/news/1993187062_1_chelsea-clinton-amy-carter-president-clinton.

8. Stephanie Petit, "Chelsea Clinton's Years in the Spotlight—From First Daughter to Mother-of-Two," People Politics, January 23, 2017, http://people.com/politics/chelsea-clinton-struggles-in-spotlight-defending-barron-trump.

9. Stephanie Petit, "Chelsea Clinton Says Barron Trump Deserves the Chance to Be a Kid," People Politics, January 23, 2017, http://people.com/politics/chelsea-clinton-says-barron-trump-defends-chance-to-be-kid.

10. Ibid.
11. Sandra Sobieraj Westfall and Tierney McAfee, "Can Chelsea Clinton and Ivanka Trump's Friendship Survive Their Parents' Presidential Bids? Chelsea Weighs In," People Celebrity, September 10, 2015, http://people.com/celebrity/chelsea-clinton-and-ivanka-trumps-friendship-how-parents-rivalry-affects-them.
12. Baer, "Making a Private Life in a Public Family."
13. Ibid.
14. Karen De Witt, "The Transition; Chelsea's School: Public or Private?" *New York Times*, December 13, 1992, http://www.nytimes.com/1992/12/13/us/the-transition-chelsea-s-school-public-or-private.html.
15. Ibid.
16. Esther Lee, "Chelsea Clinton Talks Growing Up in the White House Under 'Very Firm' Parents, Says Marriage Is 'Incredibly Important,'" *Us Weekly*, March 17, 2014, http://www.usmagazine.com/celebrity-news/news/chelsea-clinton-talks-growing-up-in-the-white-house-under-very-firm-parents-says-marriage-is-incredibly-important-2014173.

Chapter 2

1. Susan Baer, "Chelsea Clinton Decides to Attend Stanford University in the Fall: Academically Superior Institution Also Offers Refuge from the Spotlight," *Baltimore Sun*, May 1, 1997, http://articles.baltimoresun.com/1997-05-01/news/1997121159_1_chelsea-clinton-attend-stanford-university-california-campus.
2. Ibid.
3. "What Was It Like to Be at Stanford with Chelsea Clinton?" Quora, Accessed April 11, 2017, https://www.quora.com/What-was-it-like-to-be-at-Stanford-with-Chelsea-Clinton.
4. Bill Clinton, "Response to the Lewinsky Allegations," Miller Center of Public Affairs, January 26, 1998, https://millercenter.org/the-presidency/presidential-speeches/january-26-1998-response-lewinsky-allegations.
5. Peter Baker and John F, Harris, "Clinton Admits to Lewinsky Relationship, Challenges Starr to End Personal 'Prying,'"

Washington Post, August 18, 1998, http://www.washingtonpost.com/wp-srv/politics/special/clinton/stories/clinton081898.htm.

6. Todd S. Purdum, "Chelsea Clinton, Still a Closed Book," *New York Times*, June 17, 2001, http://www.nytimes.com/2001/06/17/us/chelsea-clinton-still-a-closed-book.html.

7. Ibid.

8. Sarah Lyall, "Britain Is Becoming, Chelsea Clinton Finds," *New York Times*, March 31, 2002, http://www.nytimes.com/2002/03/31/style/britain-is-becoming-chelsea-clinton-finds.html?pagewanted=all.

9. Ibid.

10. Ibid.

11. Ibid.

Chapter 3

1. Lloyd Grove, "Chelsea's Morning," *New York Magazine*, February 24, 2008, http://nymag.com/news/features/44454/index4.html.

2. Jodi Kantor, "Primed for a Second Stint as First Daughter," *New York Times*, July 31, 2007, http://www.nytimes.com/2007/07/31/us/politics/31chelsea.html.

3. Nikki Schwab, "Chelsea Clinton Was Career Confused in Her 20s," *US News & World Report*, October 17, 2013, https://www.usnews.com/news/blogs/washington-whispers/2013/10/17/chelsea-clinton-was-career-confused-in-her-20s.

4. Ibid.

5. Ibid.

6. "Leadership Team," Clinton Foundation, Accessed April 11, 2017, https://www.clintonfoundation.org/clinton-global-initiative/about-us/leadership-team.

7. Schwab, "Chelsea Clinton Was Career Confused in Her 20s."

8. Kantor, "Primed for a Second Stint as First Daughter."

9. Bill Carter, "Chelsea Clinton to Report for NBC," *New York Times*, November 13, 2011, http://www.nytimes.com/2011/11/14/business/media/chelsea-clinton-hired-by-nbc-news.html.

10. Ibid.

11. Hank Stuever, "Chelsea Clinton Makes Broadcast Debut on NBC's 'Rock Center,'" *Washington Post*, December 13, 2011, https://www.washingtonpost.com/lifestyle/style/chelsea-clinton-makes-broadcast-debut-on-nbcs-rock-center/2011/12/12/gIQApql2qO_story.html?tid=a_inl&utm_term=.8c69b2990bff.

12. David Zurawik, "Chelsea Clinton Fails Journalism 101 Again on NBC's Rock Center," *Baltimore Sun*, February 16, 2012, http://www.baltimoresun.com/entertainment/tv/z-on-tv-blog/bal-chelsea-clinton-fails-again-nbc-rock-center-20120216-story.html.

13. Van Meter, "Waiting in the Wings."

14. Ibid.

15. Ibid.

16. Maria Russo, "Chelsea Clinton's 'It's Your World,'" *New York Times*, September 14, 2015, https://www.nytimes.com/2015/09/14/books/review/chelsea-clintons-its-your-world.html.

17. Kevin Nance, "Chelsea Clinton on 'It's Your World,'" *Chicago Tribune*, September 11, 2015, http://www.chicagotribune.com/lifestyles/books/ct-prj-chelsea-clinton-its-your-world-20150911-story.html.

18. Ibid.

Chapter 4

1. Lauren Carroll, "Chelsea Clinton Mischaracterizes Bernie Sanders' Health Care Plan," Politifact, January 14, 2016, http://www.politifact.com/truth-o-meter/statements/2016/jan/14/chelsea-clinton/chelsea-clinton-mischaracterizes-bernie-sanders-he.

2. Van Meter, "Waiting in the Wings."

3. Ibid.

4. Ibid.

5. Ibid.

6. Ibid.

7. Michelle Obama, "2016 Democratic National Convention Speech," NPR, July 26, 2016, http://www.npr.org/2016/07/26/487431756/michelle-obamas-prepared-remarks-for-democratic-national-convention.

8. Sunlen Serfaty and Eric Bradner, "Chelsea Clinton Embraces Role in Her Mother's Campaign," CNN Politics, July 28, 2016, http://www.cnn.com/2016/07/28/politics/chelsea-clinton-democratic-convention-speech.

9. Ibid.

10. Anna North, "Chelsea Clinton on the Campaign Trail," *New York Times*, February 9, 2016, https://takingnote.blogs.nytimes.com/2016/02/09/chelsea-clinton-on-the-campaign-trail/?_r=0.

11. Julia Ioffe and Annie Karni, "The Enigma of Chelsea," *Politico*, July 28, 2016, http://www.politico.com/magazine/story/2016/07/2016-chelsea-clinton-hillary-bill-influence-public-image-214115.

12. Ben Wolfgang, "High-Profile, More Popular Figures Take Hillary Clinton's Fight to Campaign Trail," *Washington Times*, September 13, 2016, http://www.washingtontimes.com/news/2016/sep/13/bill-chelsea-clinton-campaign-as-pneumonia-sidelin.

13. Van Meter, "Waiting in the Wings."

14. Kelli Bamforth, "Chelsea Clinton's Tweet About Voting for Her Mother Is So Touching," *Romper*, November 8, 2016, https://www.romper.com/p/chelsea-clintons-tweet-about-voting-for-her-mother-is-so-touching-22182.

15. Lindsey Stanberry, "Chelsea Clinton Talks to R29 About What Happens Next," *Refinery29*, January 18, 2017, http://www.refinery29.com/2017/01/135946/chelsea-clinton-new-days-resolution.

Chapter 5

1. Nance, "Chelsea Clinton on 'It's Your World.'"

2. Ibid.

3. Ibid.

4. Chelsea Clinton, "20 Years of Data, 1 Year Later: Where Are We on Gender Equality?" Mogul, March 2016, https://onmogul.com/stories/20-years-of-data-1-year-later-where-are-we-on-gender-equality-by-chelsea-clinton.

5. Ibid.

6. Ibid.

7. Francesca Bacardi, "Chelsea Clinton Opens Up About Breastfeeding Charlotte and Life as a Working Mom," E!, September 29, 2015, http://www.eonline.com/news/701064/chelsea-clinton-opens-up-about-breastfeeding-charlotte-and-life-as-a-working-mom-watch-now.

8. Dana Davidsen, "Chelsea Clinton: LGBTQ Rights 'Unfinished Business' of This Century," CNN, February 16, 2014, http://politicalticker.blogs.cnn.com/2014/02/16/chelsea-clinton-lgbtq-rights-unfinished-business-of-this-century.

9. Ibid.

10. Nick Wells, "Chelsea Clinton Pushed Hillary to Support Same-Sex Marriage," *PinkNews*, October 9, 2015, http://www.pinknews.co.uk/2015/10/09/chelsea-clinton-pushed-hillary-to-support-same-sex-marriage.

11. Felipe De La Hoz, "Chelsea Clinton Gets Personal at Downtown LGBT Center," *Observer*, April 15, 2016, http://observer.com/2016/04/chelsea-clinton-gets-personal-at-downtown-lgbt-center.

12. Wells, "Chelsea Clinton Pushed Hillary to Support Same-Sex Marriage.

13. Liam Stack, "Mike Pence and 'Conversion Therapy': A History," *New York Times*, November 30, 2016, https://www.nytimes.com/2016/11/30/us/politics/mike-pence-and-conversion-therapy-a-history.html.

14. Chris Johnson, "Chelsea Clinton: 'Ex-Gay' Therapy Most Offensive Part of GOP Confab," *Washington Blade*, July 27, 2016, http://www.washingtonblade.com/2016/07/27/chelsea-clinton-ex-gay-therapy-offensive-part-gop-convention.

15. Jordan Allen, "Chelsea Clinton at DNC: LGBT Rights Are Human Rights," *Rush Hour Daily*, July 29, 2016, http://www.rushhourdaily.com/chelsea-clinton-dnc-lgbt-rights-human-rights.

16. Kevin Sieff, "Chelsea Clinton Highlights Plight of Elephants on Visit to Reserve in Kenya," *Washington Post*, May 3, 2015, https://www.washingtonpost.com/world/africa/chelsea-clinton-highlights-plight-of-elephants-on-visit-to-reserve-in-kenya/2015/05/03/13014e76-edf8-11e4-8050-839e9234b303_story.html?utm_term=.ab5fc5279a17.

Chapter 6

1. Nivea Serrao, "Chelsea Clinton Announces New Picture Book, *She Persisted*," *Entertainment Weekly*, March 16, 2017, http://ew.com/books/2017/03/16/chelsea-clinton-she-persisted-picture-book.

2. Aaron Blake, "Chelsea Clinton Finally Finds Her Political Voice—and It's Edgy," *Washington Post*, February 3, 2017, https://www.washingtonpost.com/news/the-fix/wp/2017/02/03/chelsea-clinton-unplugged/?utm_term=.69f04a15bc02.

3. Amie Parnes, "Chelsea Clinton Fuels Speculation of Political Run," *Hill*, March 15, 2017, http://thehill.com/homenews/campaign/324008-chelsea-clinton-fuels-speculation-of-political-run.

4. Hannah Thomas-Peter, "Chelsea Clinton Urges Young People to Vote," Sky News, March 9, 2015, http://news.sky.com/story/chelsea-clinton-urges-young-people-to-vote-10368465.

5. Parnes, "Chelsea Clinton Fuels Speculation of Political Run."

6. Adam Carlson, "Hillary Clinton Talks Parenting for Mother's Day: 'Watching Chelsea Mother Charlotte Is Just the Greatest Joy,'" *People*, May 7, 2016, http://people.com/celebrity/hillary-clinton-and-chelsea-talk-parenting-charlotte-for-mothers-day.

7. Ibid.

8. "About Us," Alliance for a Healthier Generation, Accessed March 22, 2017, https://www.healthiergeneration.org/about_us.

9. Heidi Stevens, "Glamour Salutes Women of the Year in Exhilarating Fashion," *Chicago Tribune*, November 11, 2014, http://www.chicagotribune.com/lifestyles/ct-glamour-women-of-year-awards-balancing-20141111-column.html.

10. Michelle Cottle, "Being Chelsea Clinton," *Atlantic*, July/August 2016, https://www.theatlantic.com/magazine/archive/2016/07/being-chelsea-clinton/485627.

11. Ibid.

12. Ibid.

13. Ibid.

14. Ibid.

GLOSSARY

affidavit A written statement, taken under oath, that can be used as evidence in court.

alma mater The school a person once attended.

barring Excluding or leaving out.

Benghazi A 2012 attack against two US government facilities in Benghazi, Libya. As secretary of state at the time, Hillary Clinton took responsibility for the lack of security at the attacked facilities.

conversion therapy Psychological treatment or counseling that aims to change a person's homosexual or bisexual orientation to heterosexual.

didactic In a teaching manner.

electoral vote The votes gathered from the Electoral College—a group of 538 electors from the fifty states that ultimately determine who will win the presidency.

gubernatorial Relating to the governor or the office of the governor.

hedge fund A partnership of investors who use high-risk investment methods to try to earn large profits.

LGBTQ Stands for "lesbian, gay, bisexual, transgender, queer." It is a more inclusive way to refer to members of the gay community.

millennials In general, people born between the early 1980s and the mid-1990s to early 2000s.

misogynist A person who dislikes or is prejudiced against women.

mudslinging Attempting to damage a person's reputation by insulting them or making accusations against them.

narcissist A person who admires himself or herself excessively.

pedigree A person's ancestry, usually from the upper classes.

poaching Illegal hunting of an animal.

Ponzi scheme A type of fraud in which investors put money into a nonexistent enterprise and see quick returns paid from money put in by later investors (rather than money generated by actual profits).

popular vote All voters in all states. In the 2016 election, Hillary Clinton won the popular vote, but Donald Trump won the electoral vote—thus, he won the presidency.

provost An administrative officer in a college or university.

silver spoon A slang term for a privileged upbringing. People born into rich families are sometimes said to have been "born with a silver spoon."

syndicate A group of individuals or organizations that are promoting a common interest.

trafficking Illegal dealing or trading.

FURTHER INFORMATION

Books

Clinton, Chelsea. *It's Your World: Get Informed, Get Inspired and Get Going!* New York: Philomel Books, 2015.

Lewis, Barbara A. *The Teen Guide to Global Action: How to Connect with Others (Near and Far) to Create Social Change.* Minneapolis: Free Spirit Publishing, 2007.

Thompson, Laurie Ann. *Be a Changemaker: How to Start Something That Matters.* New York: Simon Pulse/Beyond Words, 2014.

Websites

The Clinton Foundation
https://www.clintonfoundation.org

The Clinton Foundation website allows users to explore various issues and become involved in various initiatives.

DoSomething.org
https://www.dosomething.org/us/campaigns

DoSomething.org is an organization for youth and teens who want to make change locally and globally.

Global Changemakers
http://www.global-changemakers.net

Global Changemakers is an organization that empowers young people to work for social change.

No Ceilings: The Full Participation Project
http://www.noceilings.org

The No Ceilings Project is an initiative of the Clinton Foundation that aims to promote the full participation of girls and women around the world through various partnerships.

TakingITGlobal
http://www.tigweb.org/index.html?width=1024

TakingITGlobal is a project that empowers teens to take on social change.

Video

In the Arena: Chelsea Clinton at TEDxTeen 2013
https://www.youtube.com/watch?v=KINIDSGxKfk

In this TED talk, Chelsea Clinton talks to teens about making a difference.

BIBLIOGRAPHY

Allen, Jordan. "Chelsea Clinton at DNC: LGBT Rights Are Human Rights." *Rush Hour Daily*, July 29, 2016. http://www.rushhour daily.com/chelsea-clinton-dnc-lgbt-rights-human-rights.

Aridi, Sara. "Chelsea Clinton to Publish Children's Book, 'She Persisted.'" *New York Times*, March 16, 2017. https://www. nytimes.com/2017/03/16/books/chelsea-clinton-to-publish-childrens-book-she-persisted.html.

Bacardi, Francesca. "Chelsea Clinton Opens Up About Breastfeeding Charlotte and Life as a Working Mom." E! News, September 29, 2015. http://www.eonline.com/news /701064/chelsea-clinton-opens-up-about-breastfeeding-charlotte-and-life-as-a-working-mom-watch-now.

Baer, Susan. "Chelsea Clinton Decides to Attend Stanford University in the Fall: Academically Superior Institution Also Offers Refuge from the Spotlight." *Baltimore Sun*, May 1, 1997. http://articles.baltimoresun.com/1997-05-01/ news/1997121159_1_chelsea-clinton-attend-stanford-university-california-campus.

———. "Making a Private Life in a Public Family: Clintons Shield Chelsea from Spotlight." *Baltimore Sun*, July 6, 1993. http://articles.baltimoresun.com/1993-07-06/news/199 3187062_1_chelsea-clinton-amy-carter-president-clinton.

Baker, Peter, and John F. Harris. "Clinton Admits to Lewinsky Relationship, Challenges Starr to End Personal 'Prying.'" *Washington Post*, August 18, 1998. http://www. washingtonpost.com/wp-srv/politics/special/clinton/stories/ clinton081898.htm.

Bingham, Amy. "Chelsea Clinton's Childhood: No Pizza, Cartoons on Weekdays." ABC News, May 7, 2012. http://abcnews.go.com/blogs/politics/2012/05/chelsea-clintons-childhood-no-pizza-cartoons-on-weekdays.

Blake, Aaron. "Chelsea Clinton Finally Finds Her Political Voice—and It's Edgy." *Washington Post*, February 3, 2017. https://www.washingtonpost.com/news/the-fix/wp/2017/02/03/chelsea-clinton-unplugged/?utm_term=.69f04a15bc02.

Callahan, David. "What the Heck Does the Clinton Foundation Actually DO?" *Inside Philanthropy*, June 23, 2016. https://www.insidephilanthropy.com/home/2016/6/23/what-the-heck-does-the-clinton-foundation-actually-do.html.

Carroll, Lauren. "Chelsea Clinton Mischaracterizes Bernie Sanders' Health Care Plan." Politifact, January 14, 2016. http://www.politifact.com/truth-o-meter/statements/2016/jan/14/chelsea-clinton/chelsea-clinton-mischaracterizes-bernie-sanders-he.

Carter, Bill. "Chelsea Clinton to Report for NBC." *New York Times*, November 13, 2011. http://www.nytimes.com/2011/11/14/business/media/chelsea-clinton-hired-by-nbc-news.html.

Clinton, Bill. "Response to the Lewinsky Allegations." Miller Center of Public Affairs, January 26, 1998. https://millercenter.org/the-presidency/presidential-speeches/january-26-1998-response-lewinsky-allegations.

Clinton, Chelsea. "Throwback Thursday: Me and My Mom, Hillary Clinton." PopSugar, August 25, 2016. https://www.popsugar.com/news/Family-Pictures-Chelsea-Hillary-Clinton-42038620.

———. "20 Years of Data, 1 Year Later: Where Are We on Gender Equality?" Mogul, March 2016. https://onmogul.

com/stories/20-years-of-data-1-year-later-where-are-we-on-gender-equality-by-chelsea-clinton.

Clinton, Hillary. *It Takes a Village.* New York: Simon and Schuster, 1996.

Cottle, Michelle. "Being Chelsea Clinton." *Atlantic*, July/August 2016. https://www.theatlantic.com/magazine/archive/2016/07/being-chelsea-clinton/485627.

De Witt, Karen. "The Transition; Chelsea's School: Public or Private?" *New York Times*, December 13, 1992. http://www.nytimes.com/1992/12/13/us/the-transition-chelsea-s-school-public-or-private.html.

Guernsey, JoAnn Bren. *Hillary Rodham Clinton*. Minneapolis: Lerner Publishing Group, 2015.

Kahumbu, Paula, and Andrew Halliday. "Case Proven: Ivory Trafficking Funds Terrorism." *Guardian*, August 30, 2015. https://www.theguardian.com/environment/africa-wild/2015/aug/30/case-proven-ivory-trafficking-funds-terrorism.

Kantor, Jodi. "Primed for a Second Stint as First Daughter." *New York Times*, July 31, 2007. http://www.nytimes.com/2007/07/31/us/politics/31chelsea.html.

Lyall, Sarah. "Britain Is Becoming, Chelsea Clinton Finds." *New York Times*, March 31, 2002. http://www.nytimes.com/2002/03/31/style/britain-is-becoming-chelsea-clinton-finds.html?pagewanted=all.

Nance, Kevin. "Chelsea Clinton on 'It's Your World.'" *Chicago Tribune*, September 11, 2015. http://www.chicagotribune.com/lifestyles/books/ct-prj-chelsea-clinton-its-your-world-20150911-story.html.

Parnes, Amie. "Chelsea Clinton Fuels Speculation of Political Run." *Hill*, March 15, 2017. http://thehill.com/homenews/

campaign/324008-chelsea-clinton-fuels-speculation-of-political-run.

Petit, Stephanie. "Chelsea Clinton Says Barron Trump Deserves the Chance to Be a Kid." *People*, January 23, 2017. http://people.com/politics/chelsea-clinton-says-barron-trump-defends-chance-to-be-kid.

———. "Chelsea Clinton's Years in the Spotlight—From First Daughter to Mother-of-Two." *People*, January 23, 2017. http://people.com/politics/chelsea-clinton-struggles-in-spotlight-defending-barron-trump.

Pilkington, Ed. "The Joke That Should Have Sunk McCain." *Guardian*, September 1, 2008. https://www.theguardian.com/lifeandstyle/2008/sep/02/women.johnmccain.

Purdum, Todd S. "Chelsea Clinton, Still a Closed Book." *New York Times*, June 17, 2001. http://www.nytimes.com/2001/06/17/us/chelsea-clinton-still-a-closed-book.html.

Russo, Maria. "Chelsea Clinton's 'It's Your World.'" *New York Times*, September 14, 2015. https://www.nytimes.com/2015/09/14/books/review/chelsea-clintons-its-your-world.html.

Stack, Liam. "Mike Pence and 'Conversion Therapy': A History." *New York Times*, November 30, 2016. https://www.nytimes.com/2016/11/30/us/politics/mike-pence-and-conversion-therapy-a-history.html.

Wolfgang, Ben. "High-Profile, More Popular Figures Take Hillary Clinton's Fight to Campaign Trail." *Washington Times*, September 13, 2016. http://www.washingtontimes.com/news/2016/sep/13/bill-chelsea-clinton-campaign-as-pneumonia-sidelin.

INDEX

Page numbers in **boldface** are illustrations. Entries in **boldface** are glossary terms.

ABOUT THE AUTHOR

Cathleen Small is an author and editor who has written more than two dozen books for elementary, middle-school, and high-school readers. A lifelong Democrat, she followed the Clinton presidency and the 2016 Clinton campaign with interest. When she's not reading or writing, Cathleen enjoys traveling and seeing new places with her husband and two sons. Cathleen lives in the San Francisco Bay Area.